Advance Praise for *The Ultimate Sales Managers' Guide*

"When we think of practical ideas that inspire people and build businesses, we think of John Klymshyn. Readers of *The Ultimate Sales Managers' Guide* will learn, laugh, and be thankful for this useful, timeless tool."

> —Guy Alvarez
> Founder, Business Development Institute

"John Klymshyn writes from the trenches and leads from the front. He has distilled the most important points of sales management down to easily referenced action items that you can use right now. *This is the single most important sales management book in print.*"

> —Dave Lakhani
> CEO of Bold Approach, Inc. and author of
> *Persuasion: the Art of Getting What You Want* and
> *The Power of an Hour*

"Outstanding! This book is a bible for sales managers. It provides a foundation for anyone to build a winning team."

> —Tim Pulte
> Executive Managing Director, GVA Smith Mack

"Klymshyn's passion for people and the subject run through the entire book. Readers will get practical advice that, if taken, will ensure they realize their full sales management potential."

> —Catherine MacDonagh
> Founder, Legal Sales and Services Organization

"John Klymshyn is motivational, inspiring, and most of all practical. His focused and fun approach is the leverage every sales manager needs to help build game winning teams."

> —Joe Sciolla
> Managing Partner, CRESA Partners, Boston LLC

"John Klymshyn grabs your attention from the first page and more importantly, keeps it! This book is motivational and compelling. It's an easy read, filled with humor and practical experience. Anyone who deals with salespeople regularly should read it *immediately*."

> —Toni Jacaruso
> Vice President of Sales and Marketing,
> Dimension Development Co., Inc.

"As always, John's work is insightful, humorous, and a pleasure to read. He truly understands the rewards, frustrations, and excitement, of what it is like to manage salespeople *all day, every day*."

> —B. Tod Hughes
> President, Avison Young Commercial Real Estate, Calgary

"Klymshyn's '52 Attributes of The Ultimate Sales Manager' offer a structure and discipline for real success."

> —Linda Carchidi
> President, JFC Staffing Associates

"John Klymshyn is the world authority on the subject of sales management!"

> —Bonnie Cox
> Vice President of Organizational Development,
> Select Personnel Services, and author of
> *52 Secrets to Being the Best Employee Ever*

THE ULTIMATE SALES MANAGERS' GUIDE

THE ULTIMATE SALES MANAGERS' GUIDE

JOHN KLYMSHYN

WILEY

John Wiley & Sons, Inc.

Published by John Wiley & Sons, Inc., Hoboken, New Jersey.
Published simultaneously in Canada.

For general information on our other products and services or for technical support, please contact our Customer Care Department within the United States at (800) 762-2974, outside the United States at (317) 572-3993 or fax (317) 572-4002.

Wiley also publishes its books in a variety of electronic formats. Some content that appears in print may not be available in electronic books. For more information about Wiley products, visit our web site at www.wiley.com.

Library of Congress Cataloging-in-Publication Data:

Klymshyn, John.
    The ultimate sales managers' guide / John Klymshyn.
            p.   cm.
    Includes index.
    ISBN-13: 978-0-471-97318-8 (cloth)
    ISBN-10: 0-471-97318-1 (cloth)
1. Sales management—Handbooks, manuals, etc.   2. Selling—Handbooks, manuals, etc.   I. Title.
    HF5438.4.K55 2006
    658.8' 1—dc22

                                                                                                          2006009975

Printed in the United States of America.

10   9   8   7   6   5   4   3   2   1

CONTENTS

Part I   Finding, Keeping, and Releasing Salespeople

Part II   Sales Meetings

FOREWORD

For as long as there have been products and services to sell, there have been salespeople. For as long as there have been salespeople, there have been sales "gurus" who have sought to teach these salespeople what it takes to succeed. Thankfully for those of us who call sales our "turf," John Klymshyn truly understands the distinction between selling and successful selling. In his first work, *Move the Sale Forward*, John demonstrated his fluency with the specific skills necessary for salespeople to make deals happen.

Now, with *The Ultimate Sales Managers' Guide*, John has once again offered his unique and proven perspective on results-oriented, truly measurable success in sales management. The Ultimate Sales Manager™ as a concept is long overdue, as it is directly aimed at making you (and me), the sales leader, victorious not only in closing deals but also on an even grander scale by teaching us the skills necessary to surround ourselves with successful salespeople.

If you've ever tried to sell anything, you know how difficult it can be. To try to teach others how to be successful in selling is far more difficult, which explains why no one, until now, has effectively ventured where John's *The Ultimate Sales Managers' Guide* dares to go.

Successful selling, that is, not merely meeting one's quotas or goals consistently, but regularly blowing those goals away, has been described as an art, a skill, a compulsion (yes, a compulsion), just to name a few descriptors. When reading *The Ultimate Sales*

Managers' Guide you, as a leader of salespeople, learn the single skill that makes John Klymshyn's approach so unique. You will clearly discern that successfully managing salespeople is (more than anything else) a passion.

While reading this book, you learn about the multitude of sales personalities that exist in our world today. You also learn how many of your own past experiences in life have a direct relationship to your success in the world of selling. By understanding how these experiences can help to shape your own personal success, you will learn how to more effectively surround yourself with peers and subordinates, and effectively ensure not only their own individual success but also the success of the entire sales organization that you manage.

Why is John Klymshyn's approach so different? It is because of his passion for our craft. We have all worked with sales professionals who know the basic skills, yet who aren't ultimately successful. It doesn't seem logical that if one performs the skills that all agree are required to complete a task, that success should not be guaranteed. Yet, sales is that unique animal that requires more than simple completion of assigned tasks. As you read *The Ultimate Sales Managers' Guide*, you will easily (and enjoyably) be able to understand how the infusion of passion into the sales manager's work has everything to do with that sales manager's ultimate success.

Ask sales managers how much time they spend actually "selling," and you'll get varying answers. Some will tell you that they sell when they're not participating in in-house meetings, others will tell you that they sell when they're not reviewing the performance of those sales professionals who report to them, and still others will tell you that they simply don't have nearly enough time in their day to actually "sell." When you read *The Ultimate Sales Managers' Guide*, you will learn one of the mainstays of John Klymshyn's unique approach to our trade: Everything that we do is selling or presenting. As someone who has worked in this industry for nearly 25 years, I can tell you that there is no greater truth than this. Results for the most effective sales manager are measured in the productivity of his or her sales organization, until everyone in that organization fully understands that everything he or she does is selling, the team cannot possibly fulfill its potential for success.

Sales managers rely on many skills to achieve success. Many of these skills are learned as these managers have come up through the ranks, having "beaten the streets," having "cold-called via the phone book," and so on to earn their stripes. John Klymshyn's *The Ultimate Sales Managers' Guide* respects all of these formative experiences and makes a powerful case for the argument that the truly unique sales manager ("ultimately successful") is successful because of his or her commitment not only to basic skills, but because of his or her respect and appreciation for basic human nature. The salespeople who make up a sales organization are just that—people who sell.

The Ultimate Sales Managers' Guide powerfully relates everyday experiences in a sales organization which, when properly managed, form the building blocks for a dynamically successful sales team. John Klymshyn's insight into the dynamics of a true sales leader, honed from 20-plus years of direct personal experience, create a unique reading experience that offers the potential for winning measurable results for us all.

After all, for the Ultimate Sales Manager, aren't results what it's all about?

D. C. BECKER
Senior Vice President of Sales and Marketing
Wyndham Hotels and Resorts

April 2006

ACKNOWLEDGMENTS

This book took 15 years to think about, 2 weeks to write a proposal for, and over 7 months to type, edit, and prepare for publication. Over the years that I have practiced, studied, made mistakes, tried and rejected various sales management theories and techniques, I have come to accumulate not just experience but *wisdom*.

I have fired people, made friends, and (according to some very appreciative salespeople) changed many lives for the better. *What a great feeling.*

As I write this, we are but a few weeks away from the final version of the book having all of the parentheses put in the proper place, the quotes being verified and credited, and the cover of the book being designed and decided on.

Throughout this entire process, there have been people involved who have played a large role in getting this book into your hands. I offer my profound gratitude to:

- ◆ Dave Lakhani for opening a very wide door
- ◆ Matt Holt for the vision that preceded everything
- ◆ Shannon Vargo for guidance and encouragement
- ◆ Mark Gillet for relentless protection and dry humor
- ◆ Ivy Kagan Bierman for her passion for the process
- ◆ Kelly Kamm for the technology to make amazing connections
- ◆ The people I quote in this book

- John Elston, Michael Erickson, Marty Almquist, and Mike Ohmes for ideas and wisdom that shaped the voice of this book
- My family:
  —Terri Lynn for making 22 years too short a time
  —Lauren Marie for teaching me determination
  —John III for making writing look easy

ABOUT THE AUTHOR

John Klymshyn is the author of over 100 magazine, Internet, and trade articles on the topics of sales, business development, communication skills, and management.

A Google search of Klymshyn currently nets over 600 individual hits.

Klymshyn's first book, *Move the Sale Forward*, outlined a specific, repeatable approach to selling that has been adopted by many Fortune 500 companies.

Klymshyn is a lifelong student of the art of communication and spends his time traveling the world speaking specifically about *Moving Conversations Forward*,™ his trademarked process for sales, parenting, leadership, management, and communication skills.

John has been a guest speaker at classes and extension offerings at University of Southern California, New York University, Antelope Valley College, Woodbury University, and the University of California at Los Angeles.

He logs over 125,000 flight miles per year, bringing his message to international audiences. He has taught, coached, and consulted with firms in industries as far ranging as commercial real estate, staffing, advertising, resort and conference center management, travel, publishing, Internet services, and high technology.

Klymshyn is a New York native. He and Terri (his wife of 22 years) currently divide their time between their home in Valencia, California, and Europe.

Their two children attend college and regularly raid their parents' refrigerator.

John's passion is writing, and he is preparing a novel for publication.

His hobbies include music, reading, and traveling with his family.

INTRODUCTION

D on't read this book. Please don't *just* read it. Take it, absorb it, apply what you find, test the ideas and concepts, come back and find more, put the book down again, and go back to work.

Do not just read this book. Dive in! The title, the subject matter, or a personal recommendation put this book in your hands, and now it is decision time. It's time for you to decide how the cosmic accident of you holding this book right now will influence the rest of your life.

I know it will make an impact if you do read, try, practice, and apply the subject material. But I am not the issue. *You*, your career, and success as a sales manager are.

Let's clarify: You *should* read this book if you:

- ♦ Currently have a business card with the title sales manager, vice president of sales, director of sales, or any other title that indicates that people who sell report to you
- ♦ Currently run a team of people responsible for generating revenue for your company (whether through inbound or outbound activity)
- ♦ Are considering getting into sales management because of the career trajectory it offers
- ♦ Are a college student, working on a degree in management, and your professor talks about sales *a lot*
- ♦ Are a corporate executive, and want to know how to develop your sales manager (or managers)

- Are on a path to, or hope one day to hold, the title of vice president of sales
- Own or run a company that is struggling with developing, implementing, or maintaining a sales system and structure

Sales is the engine of any capitalist society. Nothing happens until someone sells something. But who directs, inspires, develops, instructs—in a word, *leads*—the people who make the economy run? Sales managers.

Sales managers are the great, unsung corporate heroes who make a company's promises to Wall Street come true.

Sales management is the most misunderstood (and poorly prepared for) professional position in business today.

Managing salespeople has been compared with wrestling with ocean waves, herding cats, or disciplining bees for not flying in single file. In a word—*impossible*.

The two concepts of *sales* and *management* come from such different backgrounds, and carry such unrelated motivators, that many scratch their heads and wonder, "Can the task can be *Learned? Defined? Mastered?*"

I say, "Yes!"

My favorite metaphor for the profession is "herding cats."

Imagine about 30 or 40 cats—regular, domestic, aloof, skittish—all in one backyard, all spooked by the smallest snap of a twig. Now imagine that it is *your job* to get them all into the house, without stepping on any of them, without any of them bumping into each other, and all of this happening in an orderly manner.

You may be thinking, "Good Luck."

Well, that is exactly my point. Sales management is the impossible profession, which is exactly what attracts some of the smartest, funniest, most energetic, and most determined people I have ever met to its ranks.

So, here's what you and I are going to do, now that I know I have your attention. We are going to grab that impossible task and examine it very closely to see what it requires and what it offers. We are going to determine how to make it work very effectively. From there, you and I will travel across many miles and into a unique group of minds to find not only how to succeed but also how to become The Ultimate Sales Manager.

How does that sound?

If you see this as a challenge, then you are correct. The title, the subject matter, and everything you will find on the following pages will be a consistent and continual challenge to how you think, speak, carry yourself, perform, lead, and live.

Sales management is not for the squeamish or the weak in spirit. Becoming a sales manager is the closest a person can come to embarking on an enterprise that is nearly impossible.

I cannot say that sales management is the most dangerous job because I remember how dangerous the work performed by my fellow sailors on the flight deck of the *USS Constellation* was when we were at sea, launching and landing planes in the middle of the Indian Ocean, all day and all night.

I can't say it is the hardest job because it is not as physically demanding as building houses or loading bricks.

Neither can I say that it is the most mentally challenging or stressful because you are not holding another human being's life in the balance, via a scalpel and a surgical team.

Here's the good news: If you have ever thought that you could do something that most people could not, *you are reading the right book.* Keep reading, and join me in setting a new standard that will define you, define your organization, and positively change the relationships you have with anyone who will ever report to you in a sales capacity.

Throughout this book, you learn how to take on the challenge of doing an impossible job and making results probable, achievement tangible, and work for you and your team *fun.*

If you are standing in a bookstore, considering buying this, or if you are a college student learning about what managing salespeople is all about, then welcome. I am glad to have you.

If you are currently someone who manages some of the most fascinating, challenging, and rewarding types of humans to manage, then I extend a handshake and welcome to you, as well.

If you are someone who is considering how to help the team of managers that reports to you, jump on board.

Every journey begins with a single step.
                    —Ancient proverb (possibly Chinese)

I cannot pinpoint the exact, single step that started me on the journey toward the writing of this book. As a career seller, manager, trainer, and student, I guess it started when I first thought about the fact that there must be right ways to do this job. While I was assembling some of the material for *The Ultimate Sales Managers' Guide*, I realized that this book is both the endpoint of one journey, and the beginning of a much greater one. You and I, and everyone else who reads and applies one or many of the ideas found herein will be on the greater journey together.

My journey toward the first, fiftieth, and final page of this book started in Encino, California, when I was first offered a job with the title sales manager.

I was not sure what I was getting into, but I was a cocky young guy who had closed a few deals as a desk salesperson, and of course felt that moving into management was not only logical but also probably overdue.

What makes us think that we can manage this unique creature called the salesperson? What makes us want to? Part of it is the overwhelming challenge. Part of it is the feeling that we might be able to help people improve and thrive within their sales abilities, and to get consistent, long-term results. I think a large part of it is the unannounced, unexplained journey we take.

As I indicated earlier, I really had no idea that this book was in me, until Dave Lakhani, a speaker, author, and friend, asked me where I wanted to go with my career. We talked about where I had been as a professional, father, and husband. We talked about where I had been in the creation and delivery of sales training material that I had created and trademarked for salespeople. Then he looked at me and asked, "So, what will your next book be about?"

I had been so focused on other aspects of my life that I had not even given another book any consideration. I took the next few days to think about who I was, what I was passionate about, and who I spent most of my time with. What could I write about with passion, credibility, insight, and unique perspective?

Since I spent most of my professional time selling to, coaching, and just talking with people who managed sales teams and sales forces (A team is a small, local group of salespeople. A force is a large, widely distributed group.) I thought, "Well, what do we talk about most often?"

The answer came to me before I even finished the question: Sales managers, vice presidents, presidents, and owners all ask, talk about, consult, and agonize over the following:

♦ How can I keep my individual people focused?
♦ How can I have my folks make the group goals as important to the sales individual as their personal goals?
♦ How can I become a better sales manager (i.e., what will develop my leadership, hiring, disciplining, training, and coaching skills—and anything else that will develop my people into more consistent earners, good representatives of our company in the marketplace, and good team members—and help me identify future sales managers)?
♦ What are people in similar positions (sales managers, vice presidents, and presidents) in my industry (or others), doing that would be useful and relevant to me?
♦ Where do I find the time to do the most important things in my job description?
♦ How do I communicate my expectations clearly and often enough?
♦ How can I keep my numbers consistent?

These along with many other questions are tackled in this book.

So, what does this have to do with our journey? It has everything in the world to do with it. It occurred to me, during one of the many fascinating interviews that I conducted in preparing this book, that I had actually been preparing to write it for about 15 years. Good news for you, and good news for me. So, immediately, we have something in common.

Another journey that I was unknowingly on was the one that led me to being a conduit, or a "hub of the wheel," for a unique and eclectic assemblage of intellect, talent, knowledge, and experience. The people who contributed to the creation of what you are holding in your hand had you in mind when they agreed to share the ideas and truisms that you find throughout this book.

You hear from people in business-to-business sales across such varied industries as Internet advertising sales to staffing and employment. You read the habits and techniques applied by leaders from commercial real estate to resort and hospitality sales. You hear from people who have similar personalities and ways of looking at the world as you, as well as folks with widely varying views from your own.

As the hub of the wheel, I came to realize that I had positioned myself rather well, considering that I did not plan to position myself at all. As a speaker and trainer, I picked some vertical markets to attack, to see if I could sell to them—a basic approach to building a business. Thankfully, I was fortunate enough to make a living as a result. What I was not prepared for was how I ended up developing some of the most rewarding friendships of my life.

As the hub of the wheel, I have been able to introduce people to each other who otherwise would never have met. Some of them have hired each other, either as employer/employee, or as purveyors of a product or service. They have bought from each other. That's cool, as far as I am concerned.

The journey you are now on (that is an assumptive close: I talk as if you are already committed) cannot be taken, unless you accept the ultimate challenge.

I challenge you *not* to be a good sales manager.

I challenge you *not* to be a very good sales manager.

I challenge you, right here, immediately, to aspire to, and begin working toward becoming:

The Ultimate Sales Manager

Think you are up to the task? Think you can hold your own among the top minds in the country? Do you want to do something that most people simply cannot do? Are you prepared to think, plan, work, attempt, make a mistake, attempt again, and ultimately (no pun intended) see *amazing results*?

If your answer is *yes*, then once again, *welcome*. Long journeys may begin with a single step, but the journeys that I look back on with the fondest memories are those that I have shared with someone.

I make the claim here and now that when you implement the ideas you find here, you will change, improve, and influence what you do and how you do it. I also hereby claim that when you implement what is advised, your final, measurable results will increase by many, many multiples as compared with the price you find on the cover.

Your journey must have a hoped for destination. Think for a moment about what you want to say 12 months from today about what you and your team have accomplished. Write it down on the inside cover of this book, so that the two are inexorably linked.

Once you finish the book, I ask you to reread what you wrote, to see if you might want to adjust (read, *increase*) that goal.

The book is designed to encourage regular use. There are four parts. Each part has chapters that are linked or related. Each chapter takes you a distance further toward you claiming the title, The Ultimate Sales Manager.

Throughout the book, you read interviews in which successful leaders, managers, and owners of flourishing companies offer snippets of attributes, characteristics, and habits of The Ultimate Sales Manager.

We will not draw you a picture, but we will create a mythical character. We will choose, together, to identify with that character, and compare ourselves to The Ultimate Sales Manager.

I love acronyms, and would really like it if The Ultimate Sales Manager had a better-sounding word that it created, but that can be part of the fun. Go ahead and pronounce the acronym: TUSM. Sounds like an antacid, right?

Well, that's okay. A little silliness goes a long way. One of the attributes of TUSMs (okay, I will write it out: The Ultimate Sales Manager) is a sense of humor.

A mythical character often has unusual powers, or an impossible task against insurmountable odds. That is you. A mythical character is someone who is seen as a bit different by everyone who meets, hears about, or learns from them. That is you. A mythical character wins through skill, determination, and a romantic ideal. These characters have a strong sense of what is right, the willingness and preparation to pay the price to do the right thing, and *ultimately succeed* at achieving their goals. That is *you*.

Turn the page to familiarize yourself with the structure of the book by going through the outline. Use this book—don't just read it. Make notes in the columns, highlight passages, and reference the folks quoted here in your meetings and interactions with the people you lead.

I am thrilled to begin this journey with you.

PART I

Finding, Keeping, and Releasing Salespeople

HIRING

Vision Precedes Everything

—John Klymshyn

I recently coached a salesperson over the phone, and I wanted her to understand the importance of knowing where she wanted to take her business. This is relevant to you, The Ultimate Sales Manager, because you buy and sell all day. You buy the corporate vision, and then repackage and sell it to your immediate reports.

You must start everything with a specific vision, and that must be in place and clear before you think about hiring. Do not look to fill out your head count.

Clarify and commit to a vision of your group, and hire to fulfill that vision. In this chapter and throughout this section, we talk about the employment cycle that people will have with you and your company. What do you want people to think of or speak about when they describe the environment you create on the sales floor or throughout the office? You create and significantly contribute to this environment: Know where you want the car to go before you start driving.

Some sales managers are interested in fostering healthy competition. Others want a fast-paced environment. Others are looking for their folks to show and offer mutual respect. You may think that all of these either characterize what you want or specifically describe what you have.

In my travels (I visit about 40 different corporations per year), I have developed an ability to sense the mood, environment, and culture of an office within 15 minutes of my arrival. I can tell if people are on edge, or if they are cocky. I can tell if people work together, or if they create and maintain fiefdoms.

Many of the contributors to this book have some of the best-run operations I have seen or experienced. You walk into their office, and from the first person you encounter, you know that the office is prepared, professional, and productive. Not only that, but the manager's personality is stamped on each person. People like to work for someone who knows where he or she is going.

**Attribute 1: The Ultimate Sales Manager
understands, and communicates consistently,
that vision precedes everything.**

THE THREE Ps

Strong performers must exhibit these three characteristics consistently, they must be:

1. Prepared
2. Professional
3. Productive

The three Ps establish a foundation for how you, The Ultimate Sales Manager, will run your team. This concept will appear several times throughout this book. When the three Ps are arranged in any order, they communicate great advice, and they set you and your team up for consistent success.

I am more interested in your team being consistent over time than I am in you having a great first quarter, and then falling apart for the second. This concept, this group of words, is a way to lead and, as a result, manage salespeople. I am excited to share it with you.

Now, what really excites me (and you, and anyone with whom you share this three-word concept) is that the three-P formula is like an Escher lithograph.[1] You can rearrange the components of the formula in any way you choose, and it will always make sense. (It is so amazing and inspiring to me that Escher created things and experiences that were impossible in the physical world but not in his mind or art.) The formula's varied results are what make it intriguing and powerful:

Productivity + Professionalism = Preparation
Preparation + Productivity   = Professionalism

With that in mind, let's talk about how you get to that wonderful place of having the team and environment that you want:

♦ Professional
♦ Prepared
♦ Productive

The great thing about this formula is that it allows for your personality and unique insight, and it requires those things to make the formula work.

I'd much rather have an empty seat than an empty suit.
—Thad Seligman

Translation: Don't keep people on board who are not fulfilling their commitments and quota. And when you hire, do not let an empty chair motivate you into hiring someone against your gut, or out of the profile that you will develop by the end of this chapter.

---

[1] M. C. Escher, graphic artist and visionary. He created prints and lithographs of scenes and events that were impossible in our world. He drew water going up hill, or two hands drawing each other on a page—that sort of thing. I reference his work here because most of his work can be viewed from several perspectives and still astonish the viewer. I am a big fan.

The startling truth is that empty chairs are costly. Every commercial real estate sales manager I have ever spoken to knew exactly what his "desk cost" was. This is a number that is in his budget that he must somehow earn and cover to make the office profitable. It is especially relevant to commercial real estate people because they look at everything on a "use of square footage" basis. Retail store owners can tell you what a square foot on their merchandise floor must generate *per hour*.

You should identify what it costs you to have an empty seat, and weigh that drain on the profitability of your team against the cost of leaving it empty. If each space in your office costs X dollars, you divide that among the production your team is creating, and you know what that dollar cost is.

There is another drain that is hard to put into a numerical expression:

$$Time + Effort = ???$$

If you retain people who are not working out, everyone on your team (including the guilty party) knows that they are not working out. If there is a drain on the team, it is your job to get rid of that person.

But let's think about more fun and exciting things, like the path an employee takes with you and your company.

◆

THE EMPLOYMENT CYCLE

You, The Ultimate Sales Manager, must have the vision and foresight to know if someone is going to be a good addition to your team, if an individual is already a great contributor, or if an individual needs to be removed and allowed to pursue a career goal elsewhere.

The employment cycle for salespeople starts before they join you and ends after they have been hired somewhere else. In today's competitive society, you will lose people to direct competitors, and you may find yourself being asked for an employment reference for someone who did not perform for you but who wants you to tell another employer how great an employee she was for you.

A positive aspect is that some employee's employment cycle can be as long as your tenure in your sales management position.

I have had the opportunity to read books, attend seminars, and speak directly with a lot of people about sales management. One thing that I find distracting is that I have been told many times that there are things I need to do "all the time" to be a successful sales manager. Let's agree that as a sales manager there are many things that I need to put effort into completely and consistently, but to ask me to do anything beyond breathing and thinking "all the time" is a bit ridiculous.

Now that we have that established, let's view the employment cycle that salespeople might have in your organization. In particular, let's talk about things that are going to be on your mind regularly—recruiting, interviewing, developing, coaching, measuring, rewarding, correcting, encouraging, measuring, warning, and firing.

It is tough and a bit cold to boil down the tenure of an employee to this list, but this list can save your professional life. Where are each of your folks on this list? What was the key content of the last conversation you had with everyone on the team? Warning: If you can't remember the last conversation you had with one or more of the folks reporting to you, it's time to put this book down and get to work.

Let's start with recruiting—the ongoing preparation and practice that leads to hiring.

Recruiting

Often, the employment cycle begins with the practice of recruiting. Let's lay out the eight steps as a way to help us remember them, making it easier to put them into practice:

1. Write a business plan (who, what, when, and how).
2. Identify your head count (as well as budget for salaries, bonuses, commissions, incentives, and costs of acquisition).
3. Write a job description for your sales positions.
4. Recruit to those specific job descriptions.
5. Interview.
6. Interview some more.
7. Extend offers.
8. Agree on a start date.

Before you get to a start date though, you have to recruit. Recruiting can take many forms, and you have multiple options to attract talented individuals to your team:

♦ Internet advertising (e.g., Yahoo Hotjobs).
♦ Traditional newspaper advertising.
♦ Referral bonuses for current team members: They refer someone who they think you might want to hire. If you hire that person, and they stay on board for a specific period, the person making the referral earns a bonus.
♦ Direct recruiting from other companies: You may or may not want to recruit from the competition—speaking to employees of your direct competitor opens the door for them to speak to your folks.
♦ Headhunters: These professional recruiters are paid a fee. There are also retained search companies who are paid to do the research, regardless of whether you hire the recruit. Or there are contingency firms like the one I used to work for, to which you pay a significant fee for finding someone who actually comes to work for your company.
♦ Personal recruiting from other sources: You are always on the lookout for good talent, and you may ask a waiter, a retail salesperson, or anyone else with whom you come into contact if he has ever considered working in the greatest profession in the world, and for a great company like yours.

♦ Temporary to permanent (commonly known as Temp to Perm) opportunities: I have used this, and recommend it highly. The folks who run reputable, professional temporary staffing services in your area may be able to help you with this. The concept is, you define the job requirements, and you share them with your staffing vendor. You then come to an agreement that you will interview candidates, and then the ones from that pool whom you choose, will agree to a trial employment period. This allows both you and the candidate to determine if the position you are looking to fill is a fit for everyone involved. If *yes*, you pay a fee to convert that person to full time. If *no*, you are free to release her, without the burden of an exit interview, or a long corporate process of protecting yourself from consequences. The person understands that during her temporary employment, she is auditioning for the job, and vice versa. You are auditioning to be her employer. The reason this works is that candidates like to have choices. At the same time, you get to determine if she fits because, during this period, the candidate is making an income and learning a new job, yet the staffing firm legally employs her. Look into it. It is a great thing. For an idea of firms in your area, contact my good friends at the American Staffing Association, headquartered in Alexandria, Virginia, or visit http://www.americanstaffing.net /chapters/directory.cfm.

Recruiting is an active pursuit of The Ultimate Sales Manager because you will always have an eye on the future of your head count. Salespeople may be promoted, move to other departments, or just leave.

Every seat in your office is a temporary station for your salespeople, and temporary could mean anything from a few months to many years. With an eye on the potential ebb and flow of people moving in and out over time, it is ideal to have some prospects in the wings at all times who could potentially fill an empty desk or to help staff a new branch.

Let's think of the employment cycle of salespeople as a timeline that looks like a bell curve. It moves from left to right, and each stage of the timeline takes more time and effort, so it is wider at the center (the time when the person is Prepared, Professional, and Productive). When you are recruiting, it is hard to get a sense of when the people you are most interested in will come on board, if ever. Many of the managers who I interviewed for this book had conversations with folks that they wanted to come work for them for months, even years.

Should the person work out and stay on board, she stays in the timeline's center, which is widest when she is producing. If someone is not working out, the line gets thinner because your investment of time and energy with that person diminishes. Your attention turns to documenting failures to comply or produce. Your time is involved in uncomfortable conversations about what must happen in order for the person to stay. You will have, by this time, a gut sense as to whether the person will ultimate stay and find a place on the team. When it is time to let the person go, the line thins. It could stretch out over time, however, depending on what steps and time period must be invested to satisfy corporate standards and state law before you can send employees on their way.

When we bring someone on board, it is wise to plan to spend a fair amount of time answering questions, making introductions, explaining basic procedures, and helping the new hire navigate the team and the overall company. You cannot expect someone to show up for work Wednesday, and start selling Thursday. But I am a big fan of starting people in the middle of the selling week. It allows them a few days to absorb a ton of information, followed by a weekend, before they have to get from Monday morning to Friday afternoon at a new job, in a new environment, with a new set of coworkers, and (most important) a new boss. Let them talk out the first few days with friends and family over the weekend, to make sure they come back the following Monday. That last statement is delivered a bit tongue in cheek. I have been told stories of many salespeople who start work at 8:00 A.M. on Monday, go out to lunch at noon, and never come back.

Recruiting is also a plodding, potentially long-term investment. I was recruited into two separate sales management positions by people I had done business with or known for over a year each.

Recruiting is really based on you knowing what type of individual you want, and how those various individuals you either inherit or recruit will work together to create the tangible, reliable environment that you want. I have recruited waiters and waitresses. I have recruited people who came to my office to sell me something. I have recruited from competitors, and I have recruited from companies that had nothing to do with what I sold. I have even recruited people from other departments in a company.

I found recruiting to be fun, because every environment I have endeavored to create was upbeat, lively, and there was a lot of laughing going on during the day. People in other departments notice stuff like that, and it is very flattering (and made my job a lot easier) when someone sharp, driven, hardworking, and reliable would approach me to be considered for the next available position in my department. Imagine—he wanted to leave a regular-paying job to risk working for me and making more than he ever dreamed. I have taken people from customer service jobs, from delivery jobs, from operations and administrative jobs, and provided them with a platform to change their lives forever.

I do not want to appear sappy or overly emotional, but I unapologetically embrace and enjoy people who trust their own ability enough to risk everything on themselves. This is the true test of determination and character, and it is thrilling to be a part of, and often a facilitator of, that type of life experience.

Recruiting requires you to have a clear vision, to have your eyes and ears open, and for you to be able to say no. Sales is not for everyone, and if your heart tells you loudly that someone should not do it or try it, trust your heart.

It would be wonderful if The Ultimate Sales Manager never had to recruit—if we found a few great folks and everything was just peachy all the time. Unfortunately, that is not realistic. The hope and wish is that we get to retain strong individuals.

In Chapter 5, you learn an approach for classifying your existing team. When we operate under the assumption that *vision precedes everything*, we have a vision for what the team needs. We have to fill gaps and add where necessary. We have to recognize those who may be on their way out, and as a result, we have to be smart about what level of person to bring in. By understanding how to classify the various members of the team, we are clearer on whom to hire.

The goal of recruiting is to bring more productive individuals into your already performing team. Before I hire someone to be a contributing part of that team, I want to do everything I can to see if he is prepared, professional, and productive.

Behaviorial Interviewing

Dennis Napoliello and I met when I sold him a half-day sales training seminar. At the time, he was a regional director for a wireless services provider. He now holds the title of senior director of sales for Equinox Fitness, a high-end gym and sport company based in New York. He and I come together on the hallowed ground of a shared passion: professional football. To avoid alienating anyone who is a fan of a team that may have beaten our team soundly, or to whom we might return the favor in the future, suffice it to say that we are rabid fans of a storied franchise, and leave it at that. Dennis supports Attribute 2 of The Ultimate Sales Manager.

**Attribute 2: Listen and interview well,
and know who you are hiring.**

Dennis tells us:

The biggest challenge in hiring salespeople is that there is a portion of the population that is adept at interviewing.

I am a practitioner of behavioral type questions during the interview that will tap into someone's mind.

During my years in sales management, I have interviewed recent college graduates who did not even understand what the job was, and I interviewed people who have been selling for a while, who know what questions are typically asked during a sales rep interview. Once I saw that a few times, I decided that I would ask behavioral questions.

These are designed to find out what is important to people. By working with the managers who reported to me, I did a variety of different things to develop our collective ability at interviewing and finding the best candidates for our open positions.

As an example, I did an exercise with my sales managers, where I asked them to come to me with a list of the key skills that helped someone to be successful in our business. Not necessarily sales in general—we worked to identify the keys to our industry, and the people who were successful in it.

We came up with something called the Salesperson Characteristics Model. It had 25 key skills and or characteristics of the people who worked for us and who were successful. We rated candidates on a 3-2-1 scale. A ranking of 3 was above average, 2 was average, and 1 was below average.

First, I had the managers go back and grade their own people according to this scale, so that they could identify ways to work with their current employees to make them better, and then I asked them to employ this model of grading characteristics of every person they interviewed.

So that they could take a look at it, and tally it at the end—

Say someone was a 3 on persistence, a 2 on computer skills, and a 1 on industry knowledge, and you could have someone net out at a 2.79. This would not be a guarantee, but it was a benchmark for who would be a good candidate for us.

This gave us a specific picture of who would fit into the organization. We as sales managers should think about the people we sit next to, even if they were recently promoted, and identify the best of the best and their skills. This gives us a measurement about whom we should look to hire.

The most successful person I ever hired made the grade for us, and was hired because of a combination of our identification of those graded attributes, along with behavioral interviewing, for example:

"Describe a challenge you had persuading a certain individual or group to take a specific course of action."

"Think of a time when you identified a hidden agenda. How did you identify and work through that agenda?"

The goal is to ask a question that can be answered by anyone (say, a college graduate with limited experience to a journeyman sales representative). With recent graduates, you can tailor it to their experiences with study groups or group projects; with an experienced salesperson, it can be about winning a customer—the goal is to ask questions beyond "Where do you want to be in five years?"

All this question does is get us pat answers—too often people would give me rehearsed answers. I also stay away from questions like: "What do you think you need to work on?" or "What are your weaknesses?"

Behavioral interviewing means that I am looking for a response for when they actually exhibited the behavior that I asked about.

The Ultimate Sales Manager is looking for something other than the answer to stock interview questions. Often, the intent of these questions is to get the candidate talking so that the sales manager may learn more about the candidate.

Personally, I have never been a fan of questions like "What is your goal should you come to work with us?" or "Where do you see yourself in five years?" because often the response would be: "I want your job."

I like the fact that people interviewing for a position with my company have ambition, but this doesn't tell me anything about their character or how they think. These are key points of interest for me, now, and were throughout my tenure in sales management. I mentioned this to Dennis. His response:

> Absolutely—I like questions or challenges like: "Tell me about a time that you are proud of, when you were able to recognize how another person felt, and what was the situation, and how did you handle it?"
>
> I like this, because it is a way for us to delve into what is really important to people.
>
> I remember at one point when I was in wireless services, and we were getting a lot of candidates from competitors. Many of those people were not necessarily the best for our team because they may not have measured up to our measurement criteria, as outlined in our Salesperson Characteristics Model.
>
> There are many professional interviewers, and this question always helped me—the idea is to see if people can think on their feet. Many times, it brought a smile to people's faces, other times I got the response: "No one has ever asked me that before."
>
> I ask, "Can you tell me about a time when you did something nice for someone?"
>
> Talk about a way to get someone thinking during an interview.
>
> There is a fine line between hiring someone who is like you, and someone who has similar habits and attributes.
>
> I want people with different ways of looking at things, but you must find people who are consistent. As a sales manager, you want to minimize the ups and downs of the selling life.

Developing

Dennis and I agree on many things, and most significantly on the usefulness of Attribute 3 of The Ultimate Sales Manager.

Attribute 3: Hire people you think will amaze you. Develop them into people who amaze themselves.

Very little of your day should be a surprise. Having to talk someone down after he lost a deal may happen at any time, and the fact that you know your salespeople well enough to be able to handle them individually in different situations will prepare you for more difficult conversations when situations arise.

You will recruit based on the hope that the individuals you hire will adhere to this formula. You will interview, screen in, screen out, make offers, then hire, and the employment cycle begins.

As you find them, or they find you, and you come to an agreement about their role, you offer them the growth and confidence they need to be successful, and they stay.

This is the ideal, and not entirely uncommon, experience for The Ultimate Sales Manager. Unfortunately, there is also a significant amount of time that sales managers will devote to tracking goals[2] only to then end the cycle of employment of salespeople.

So, if we look at the employment cycle from a linear, timeline perspective, we add a third dimension when the timeline is wider in the middle, with the most active, and hopefully productive, period of employment being represented by this widest part. This should be when the person is most prepared, professional, and productive. This also means that this should be when the person is making the greatest measurable contribution to the team and to your attainment of objectives.

There are just a few ways for you to acquire a team. You either build it from scratch (a lot of work, and a tremendous amount of fun), or you inherit an existing team.

---

[2] Some companies call your expected revenue attainment your "budget." Others call it "goal," and another company that I worked for called it "plan." Personally, I prefer "goal." Not because I don't think that I will make it, but because "budget" sounds like I am limited to that number. You and I can get into a discussion of semantics and stuff when we meet, but for now (the duration of this book), let's use "goal."

If you are someone who has inherited a team, there will probably be an overwhelming desire to make some changes. In my sales management career, I inherited two separate sales teams (one large, one small) at two different companies. It is difficult to step in and manage a preexisting team because there is a social momentum (or lack thereof) when you as the manager come from outside the team. Both of these teams found ways to make my job challenging, however, I learned and implemented various techniques to create team synergy, and ultimately meet revenue goals.

Outside of inheriting a team, you may have the rare opportunity to hire a team from scratch. This is very enjoyable and rewarding because you are able to imprint your personality and style on the team from the beginning. I was asked to do this for a company called Tandberg Data, when it hired me to be its inside sales manager. It had allotted office space, designed a plan for what it wanted to sell, defined to whom it wanted to sell, and determined the price at which it should sell. All that was missing was a team dedicated to the goal, and someone to create the team. It was a dream opportunity.

Tandberg had a history as a tape-recording manufacturer, and in the United States in the 1980s and 1990s, it sold high-quality tape backup drives for computer networks. To give you an idea of how long ago this was, we were selling machines that were powerfully robust—they could back up an *entire* gigabyte of information, in less than an hour.

Now, you may smile when you read this, and yes, it dates the author a bit, but at that time, this was a hot little product. Tandberg Data was competing with several other manufacturers, and the exciting part of the assignment was that Tandberg's name was largely hidden from users because the bulk of its products were sold under the traditional original equipment manufacturer (OEM) model. This meant the products were manufactured in Norway under a contract to apply the brand name and label of Company A because Company A wanted to have consistency in the branding of the entire computer network that it would deliver to its ultimate end user (customer). As an OEM, Tandberg sold the drives to IBM. Many IBM systems with a tape backup drive sold during that period had Tandberg's product, with IBM's name on the front.

Our job was different. We were to make the brand of Tandberg known to a different set of customers, on a smaller scale, yet still have enough sales to affect the factory, and pay for the existence of the department. These potential customers were called value-added resellers.

Because I had built a decent career up to that point of selling and teaching others to sell professionally over the phone, the folks at Tandberg felt that I was the best person to build the team. This is where I learned the thrill of building a team from scratch.

First, I had to define specifically what the job entailed. This meant defining my role as well as the jobs of the people who would work in the new department. I had to define what the measurement criteria would be (e.g., number of dials per day, number of contacts, number of quotes, number of trial units sent out, or number of specification sheets faxed). The measurement criterion is based on the ultimate goal but must allow you to accurately measure success, analyze areas for improvement, and track what works and what doesn't.

This is where I started to aspire to Attribute 4 of The Ultimate Sales Manager.

Attribute 4: Work to maintain high morale, through consistency, attitude, and compassion.

Establishing and inspecting measurement criteria would come to be a staple of how I taught, recruited, and managed for the balance of my career (see *Move the Sale Forward*—my book on selling).

Validating

The only way I would feel confident in labeling this book as the "ultimate guide" would be if I was convinced that the ideas and techniques offered here were proven. I feel that theory is a wonderful thing, but practical application is how things really find their validation.

In preparing for the various sections and chapters, I conducted over 30 hours of interviews with people (like Dennis Napoliello—smart, driven, sales managers or leaders with a successful track record) who you hear from in the following pages. It is my sincere hope that while you read this book, and in the future, you use much of the enclosed advice to develop your style, achieve your goals, and ultimately (you will see that word a lot here) recruit, train, and manage other sales managers.

Richard Warshauer is a career sales manager in the commercial real estate industry. Currently, Richard is the sales manager for GVA Williams, a highly respected New York City firm. Richard has interviewed thousands, and hired and managed hundreds, of sales professionals in his illustrious career. When I spoke to him about hiring, he told me:

> The first step is to do your business plan: What sort of people are you seeking and what do you expect them to do? Write a realistic job description and forecast your head count. Sharpen your job description to the exact needs of your company at that time, but always look to the future.
>
> Of course, you will always want to recruit candidates with certain personality traits and mental abilities that mirror your organization's core competencies. Appearance and communication skills are always critical, as well as the candidate's meshing with your corporate ethos. In addition to the basic passion and sales drive that we look for in every person, we also place great importance on integrity and team play.

Richard's advice is useful, because he makes us look at the continuum of what we described earlier as the bell-curve view of a salesperson's employment cycle. Mr. Warshauer admonishes us to prepare and be professional so that we can continue to be productive.

Ed Friedman, executive vice president and principal of Global Brokerage and Advisory Services, with Newmark Knight Frank, agrees:

> We have to be introspective. A hire is not made in a vacuum. It should be tied to goals and objectives of an organization. Is your sales team (or force) mature in all markets?
>
> Are you introducing a new product? Is the organization in a growth or contraction mode? Are you publicly traded? What is the structure (e.g., partnership or C corp)?
>
> Hiring has a direct nexus to any organization's value proposition.
>
> I ask everyone in our organization, after interviewing a candidate, to be able to come back to me with feedback and answers to the following:
>
> ♦ What initial feel do you get from someone on a visceral basis?
> ♦ What level of vocabulary, as well as general business acumen does he demonstrate?
> ♦ What type of financial skills does the person possess?
> ♦ Is that person able to speak with expertise about cashbook and tax issues?
> ♦ What is the quality of the persons' former representation assignments, and who did he represent?
> ♦ What role did that person play in those assignments?
>
> And is the person likeable? Is this someone you could envision having a social relationship with, *or* if not you personally, would other people want that? Is this person someone who is fun to be around?

Ed and Richard address the tangibles and intangibles in their respective interviewing approaches. They both lead teams that are in the commercial real estate industry and they are both based in New York, the largest center of commercial real estate in the United States.

Not only are they both approached often, they both have a very specific approach to the hiring and interview process. Richard limits the number of people currently on board at GVA Williams with whom a candidate will meet. Ed has the candidate meet a minimum of a dozen people at Newmark Knight Frank.

Ed tells us:

Art, science, gut, intellect, and experience each play a role in your interviewing and screening technique.

As such, we look for the following traits:

♦ Articulate
♦ Thoughtful
♦ Possesses a fantastic vocabulary
♦ Seems to be able to go with the flow

Ed feels that author and consultant David Maister "got it right." Ed wants people in his organization who are "SWANs":

Smart
Work Hard
Ambitious
Nice

Ed says:

An organization is only as good as the transgressions it accepts. We do not want people who are just hitters, who engage in activities unbecoming, and who do not reflect our core values.

When you think about your business plan, the first point to be addressed must be head count. From there, you decide what the attributes are of the people you want to fill out that head count.

Ed, and many other people I interviewed, felt that identifying someone's resilience and flexibility in an interview was essential to determine her potential as a successful member of the team.

You may not always have a choice as to who reports to you, and there have been stories of "raiding" productive sales teams in organizations to fill out the "plan" in other divisions. It is unfortunate, but it is a fact of life.

When you create a business plan, you get to draw a picture of what you want your selling year to look like and gauge your performance against what you anticipate it will be.

This leads us to the Attribute 5 of The Ultimate Sales Manager.

Attribute 5: Never ask a salesperson to do something you have not done or would not do.

This simplifies the process into specific tasks, which helps to divine action steps for the week, month, quarter, and year. The title of this chapter is not designed to oversimplify the process. Your skill and aplomb for this part of your job affects, impacts, and potentially defines every other minute of your sales management day. When you hire the wrong people, your team and the management of them is a burden. When you hire the right people, it is easier to perform the job you were hired to do.

When you are recruiting and preparing to hire, you must set the criteria in advance for people whom you want on your team. Driven, focused, humor-filled people do not fall into your lap every day, and you may have to try a few approaches, and (even more tiring) a few attempts, before you hit your stride. Recruiting is a skill that I learned over an extended period. Interviewing is just a part of it.

I spent time as a recruiter for the U.S. Naval Reserve before I did any corporate recruiting. This was during peacetime, and it was in an affluent area. My assigned goal was seven people enrolled per calendar month, and I was recruiting people who had fulfilled an agreement with any branch of the U.S. military. We referred to them as NavVets (navy veterans who had served active duty time and had received an honorable discharge) and OsVets (people who had completed an enlistment with *other* branches of the military, from the army and the marines to the air force and the coast guard).

Now (to make it more challenging), I was tasked with finding, recruiting, and enlisting people whose jobs were critical to the local mission of the U.S. Naval Reserve. This meant that I was expected and required to attract people to the service who could commit to ser-ving one weekend of every month and two full weeks of every year. We were even more specific, in that these people needed to have both skill and training that was narrowly focused. I am sure you see the parallel here, in how this prepared me to recruit per-formance-focused salespeople.

As a U.S. Naval Reserve recruiter, I was thrilled to have the job because it put me back in uniform, it gave me the opportunity to continue to serve (I had completed four years of active duty just 18 months prior), and I got to work in a pretty great environment. My territory was three California counties: Santa Barbara, San Luis Obispo, and Ventura. (I saw a fair amount of shoreline and ocean driving around these counties in my government vehicle.)

While it was exciting, it was hard, and it required a specific focus to my recruiting efforts. That the candidates were past mili-tary members was an initial qualifying criteria, but it was far from the *only* criteria. To make things more interesting, no one was obli-gated to sign up. All of these folks had served a full tour of duty or enlistment on active duty. It was strictly volunteer.

I won several awards as a U.S. Naval Reserve recruiter, and I be-lieve it was because I was focused, diligent, and really wanted peo-ple to enjoy the benefits available.

◆

Hiring and Releasing

With all this advice, I must also include a caveat: If you recruit suc-cessfully and hire the person you were looking for, it does not guar-antee his success in your organization. Make sure that if someone does not work out, you do not dwell on it. Use it, learn from it, *and move on.*

Imagine that you are a football quarterback who, during a game, will throw more than a dozen passes (maybe twice that). It is the sec-ond quarter of a tied game. You throw a pass right into the arms of a defender, and he runs the ball back for a touchdown. You are going to be back on the field almost instantly, and you must learn from that error, and move on. You must take the lesson, internalize it, make it part of your armor for the future, and go on to the next task.

Having to release someone is difficult, and it can be an emotional experience for you. It certainly will be an emotional experience for some of the people you will have to release, and in Chapter 6, we discuss what leads up to, and occurs during, that dreaded conversation.

Some might say that we should have a different personality toward such events, but I never enjoyed letting people go, and do not know many professional managers who do. It is a necessary responsibility of the job.

As we examine the trajectory of the employment cycle of a salesperson, we notice that in the beginning, everything is upbeat and positive. Your endless wellspring of positive attitude and hope for the culture will assist you at this stage of your building a team. If you have inherited a team, you must still view it as a team that you will build because your company deserves the smartest decisions and actions from you throughout your sales management day and career. It has entrusted you with the welfare of the employees, the health of the department, and the image of the company as an employer.

Do not ever lose sight of the fact that everything you do, say, imply, or promote is being watched, absorbed, and evaluated at all times by both the people who report to you, and everyone else in the company with whom those folks come into contact.

With this as an intimidating fact, let's approach hiring from the most positive, prepared, and professional view, which will inform your actions and influence your results. Results are your ultimate measurement, but your employer and staff will be very aware of and sensitive to how you achieve your results.

Hiring is not something you can always do, but it is certainly a priority for you to plan and manage. (For the duration of the book, and for every conversation you have beyond this experience, remember that my personal definition of "to manage" is *to get the most out of.*)

The character, flexibility, and productivity of your team will be affected by every staff decision you make. Whether you add a top performer, or you release someone who does not fit into your scheme, you impact the overall team, if for no other reason than simple human dynamics.

Think about it this way: You sit 14 people in a room, and ask them to introduce themselves, one by one. One of these individuals might feel pressured because she does not like speaking in front of groups. Another might want to be the comedian of the group. Yet another might be wound so tight that he wants to say the exact right thing, with the exact right delivery all the time. This desire consumes his thinking so much that when it *is* time for him to speak, he has nothing prepared.

As soon as you get halfway through the 14 introductions, two people walk into the room. You do not acknowledge them but everyone knows they are there. The difference in the atmosphere is palpable. You see people exchanging subtle signs with each other about you, the new people, other folks in the room, and so on.

Take this scenario and amplify it. When a sales team hits its stride, and there is a healthy mix of good-natured competition, there are a few laughs, there are one or two heated exchanges over territory, time off, or some professional sporting event, and you have a definable environment.

Each time you add or subtract someone from that environment, you change that. You must be sensitive to this when you hire, when you fire, and when you discipline anyone on your team. A friend of mine, Mike Barrett, once wisely told me, "Words never stop traveling at the first pair of ears."

This image has stayed with me, and it informs a note I find relevant to our conversation about finding, keeping, and releasing salespeople. You do not lead, speak, interact, or cajole in a vacuum.

The industry you sell in may be relatively small. You could be in a similar situation to Bob Dean of Grubb & Ellis: His closest competitor in his market (Sacramento, California) leases an office in the *same building* as his office. I point this out, because there is a very real possibility that the conversations he has with his people are relayed, translated, or recounted (at some level) with people who work for his (or your) competitor.

One of the places from which you will most logically recruit is your competitors. Here in the United States, we have become very fond of "noncompete" agreements. (Noncompete—a signed document entered into with the same faith and confidence as a prenuptial agreement. "I love you, and know that we will be together forever, but if you leave me, I want everything back, and then some.") It is not pleasant to lose people who are bringing in revenue, and the most logical place for them to go is to a company that sells the same thing you do. That is what competition is all about.

A common occurrence in sales organizations goes something like this: You run a business or a sales team, and that team is selling Gigabats (I like that word, because I made it up and it sounds hi-tech enough for the twenty-first century).

In selling these Gigabats, you learn that every so often, when someone on your team gets close to closing a deal, the account goes to a competitor at the last minute.

As a prepared, professional, productive sales manager—no, as The Ultimate Sales Manager—you have created contacts and sources that provide you with competitive intelligence on a regular basis. Tapping these sources, you learn that it is one particular salesperson who usually beats your folks out.

Oww. Stings a bit, doesn't it? You digest the information, talk to your friends, your spouse, and maybe even the person who cuts your hair about this fascinating fact, and someone says to you quite innocently, "Why don't you just recruit that salesperson, so your company can get those deals?"

It sounds devious yet brilliant. It sounds like you will have the opportunity to be a true competitor, because competing teams always want the best talent on their side. They want the strongest offense and the stingiest defense. And you want the revenue.

The first thing to think about is *not* the dollars, the awards and accolades, or the satisfaction of winning those next deals because you made a shrewd addition to your team. The *first thing* to think about is whether this person will strengthen, contribute to, and fit into the culture of your team, your company, and your approach to managing.

As The Ultimate Sales Manager, you are not hoping to be the most popular (although people will not continue to work for someone whom they do not like). You, The Ultimate Sales Manager, are looking to build a strong, winning team that will last more than one season.

As a result, you can rely on and relate to Attribute 6 of The Ultimate Sales Manager.

Attribute 6: Attract top talent, retain team players, appreciate the people you have, and do not delay in removing those people who do not fit.

So, I pose the following ethical question: "Is it okay to recruit talent from your competition?"

You and I can debate this when you attend one of our retreats, but you also need to wrestle an answer out of your circle of advisors and land on something not only that you are comfortable with but also that you do not feel as though you need to defend. Where will recruiting from the competition fit into your team?

So, if Tony T. is hitting it out of the park working for your competitor that is one thing. If he is taking deals away from your salespeople (and as a result your bottom line), then that is another story altogether, isn't it?

VISION PRECEDES EVERYTHING

Let's work through the answer to the following: *What does your team look, feel, and sound like?*

There are a variety of colorful phrases and axioms for how you will be measured, examined, and critiqued. Dennis Napoliello told me that he always kept the following in mind:

> As a sales manager, you are always going to be the topic of someone's dinner conversation. Either you are great because you stood up for someone today, or you are a creep because you had to redo a commission. Whatever the issue might be, you are out there, and you are going to be the topic of someone's dinner conversation that night.

With that in mind, here are some concepts and concretes to list, examine, and decide on:

♦ What is the *fun* quotient?
♦ What does it feel like to work for you?
♦ What kind of risks are your salespeople ready to take, and which ones do they feel you will support, regardless of the outcome?
♦ What do you ask them to do, at which you personally are adept?
♦ How do you attract talent (e.g., referral, recruiting, company reputation, or word of mouth)?
♦ What do you set out as the expectations for conduct, decorum, or conflict resolution?
♦ On what do you want your folks to focus?
♦ How do you want your folks to respond to competitive influence, overtures, and challenges?
♦ How do your folks think they are being measured?

All of these are part of how you are perceived in the market, because it is fascinating to me that regardless of what image I *want* to project, the image that people walk around with is the one that is the aggregate of their collected impressions of me and my company.

What they hear about how I manage, how I recruit, how I release people—all of this is out in the marketplace for all to absorb.

Thad Seligman is the president of NAI Horizon, a commercial real estate brokerage in Phoenix, Arizona. I respect Thad's opinions and ideas because he has proven his theories on the playing field, in several stints as a sales manager. Thad says:

> The personality traits that are necessary for a salesperson to be successful are innate. The technical skills can be taught to anyone. If someone does not have a competitive, "fire is burning" desire to score the point to win (those are personality traits), they will never make a salesperson.
>
> The person who traditionally identifies prospects, makes a relationship with them, and closes the sale or deal—that takes a certain type of personality—has the attributes of the sales personality, and some of those attributes are:
>
> - Goal Oriented
> - High desire to win
> - Does not naturally delegate
> - Likes to do it all
> - Not much in terms of detail
> - Lacks patience
> - High levels of energy (works long periods of time or on multiple projects)
> - People oriented
> - Several (not all) opposite personality traits from a sales manager
>
> Motivational interests are different between a sales manager and a salesperson. They have different ways to look at things. Salespeople are impatient; sales managers' ability to succeed is based on their patience with multiple personalities and people. Salespeople get satisfaction from scoring the point themselves, and they get little satisfaction from seeing someone else succeed. Sales managers cannot do that. Their success and sense of value come from seeing other people succeed. The sales manager is the director; the salesperson is the lead actor in the film.

This is why many successful salespeople who are promoted to sales manager seldom have the same success in that role compared to the success they had as salespeople. They don't have the tools to manage salespeople. They are frustrated, their needs are not being met—the salespeople are being overridden by someone who still wants to play the lead or score the point *themselves.*

Ed Friedman offers:

Sales managers must *never* hire someone like themselves—which may not be the role they are interviewing for—for the same reason that great baseball players may not make the greatest managers.

Hiring is the beginning of the climb up the mountain to becoming The Ultimate Sales Manager. It also outlines for us the importance of Attribute 7 of The Ultimate Sales Manager.

**Attribute 7: Always know what makes each
individual on your team tick.**

Hiring is beyond essential for sales managers—it is one of the biggest determinants of success or failure.

Now that you know how to hire a good person, you need to know how to train him or her. We cover this in detail in the next chapter.

2

TRAINING

As a person who has made a living as a sales trainer for some years now, this chapter holds special interest for me. My approach to management is very focused on leadership, encouragement, accountability, consequences, and rewards.

During my tenure as a sales manager, my goals were:

♦ Get the most out of my team.
♦ Maintain an emotional balance.
♦ Be consistent.
♦ Train, coach, encourage, and empower.
♦ Measure, respond, coach, and clarify expectations.

It is difficult to determine the best way to train people in the skills they need to perform many of the functions of the selling process. The most complicated step of the selling process also requires the most improvisation: the conversation.

When a salesperson cold-calls a prospect (which is the first point of contact), things can get dicey. Proper training ensures that your people represent the company appropriately, professionally, and in a friendly manner. People on your team interact with prospects and clients every day. This means that they represent you and your company. You want both potential and current customers to leave the experience with a positive image of your company. You also want the salespeople to make the most of their time and effort, and training is an ongoing priority issue for The Ultimate Sales Manager.

The first step to implementing a successful training program is to plan a training budget for your salespeople. Second, you must set aside time with each person reporting to you, to learn his or her attitudes, desires, and expectations of the training you offer or fund.

If you choose to retain an outside firm to train your salespeople, a plethora of companies and services offer a variety of programs. Sessions and classes are set up in formats from multiweek courses (meeting at the same time and place, outside of your office, with people from other companies, to cover a broad range of material) to motivational seminars to skill training.

In your budget, there must also be funding set aside for some internal training initiatives. Varied systems allow your people to think about their selling approach more and more over time. I subscribe to a simple formula: Think. Do. Win. I have even launched a web site for the public that is about success attainment at all levels, in a variety of fields. I mention this here because the simple Think-Do-Win formula applies to any training that you offer your folks.

Different resources that you can make available to your sales team include:

- *Build a lending library.* Have people sign things in and out—it creates a sense of exclusivity, and it lets you know who is interested in training, and who is not.
- *Make multiple copies of CDs and videos available for distribution.* Try not to be biased with this approach. Let your people investigate a few techniques and adopt the ones that are consistent with your corporate ethics and expectations and still get the job done. (If you come across an approach that you like, that's great—it is much more important that your salespeople identify the approach that they prefer because this is the technique they will most readily investigate, study, and apply.)

♦ *Require correspondence courses.* There are online sales courses, Dale Carnegie training, and many other ways that your sales-people can continue their professional selling education out-side the office. I suggest you investigate at least partially funding these. The challenge with outside training programs is that you have to monitor the person's attendance and par-ticipation. It is one thing to spend significant money on a training course. It is quite another to spend the money, only to find out that the salesperson did not attend any of the ses-sions. A benefit of sending people out to these types of op-portunities, however, is the wonderful experience you have when a salesperson attends, participates, and brings ideas and perspectives back to your group. These classes, because they are sold to various companies, allow the people you send to learn from people who also sell. This can be very useful.

♦ *Attend off-site generic sales training.* Many famous authors and speakers travel and lecture. Have one or more individuals from your team go to these events and bring back resources, ideas, and critiques.

♦ *Provide computer-based training.* Companies create CD-ROM or DVD-based training videos that illustrate interactivity, role playing, and other systems that encourage your people to think about their selling approach more and more over time.

♦ *Bring in outside providers.* For example, my company makes the bulk of its revenue by teaching and coaching sales managers and salespeople. Our area of expertise is in business develop-ment, relationship development, cold calling, and moving conversations forward. For more information, please visit our web site: www.generatorinc.com. Or you may call our office for referrals to other sales training providers. Our phone number is: (661) 775-9581, or you can visit our web site: www.generatorinc.com.

♦ *Recruit internal experts.* This tactic is a double-edged sword, but I like the cutting edge that this offers because when you can enlist the participation of a successful member on your team in training and developing others, two things happen. First, it shows everyone on the team that this is part of your culture. Second, it brings an expert, accomplished voice to your vision. People in your company who sell well can be your greatest resource for how to overcome common obstacles, answer questions, solve problems, or even make useful introductions. The only drawback is that being a productive, experienced salesperson (as in the earlier example presented about salespeople moving to sales management positions) does not automatically make that person a solid, reliable sales trainer. This is the other side of the double-edged sword. Make sure that *anyone* you put in front of your team has decent presentations skills, stays on point, and delivers useful information. This is not easy, but little about your job is, or will be. These folks, when properly and productively deployed, can be invaluable resources for improving company perception, providing competitive information, and designing successful approaches that you may not use but can comfortably endorse. Most of all, they give less experienced salespeople insight into what they must do, think about, and experience while becoming a successful team member.

♦ *Conduct training yourself.* This includes education about product updates, company information, new marketing initiatives, competitive information, market influences, and corporate policy and expectations. These are all part of the ongoing training that keeps your sales force informed and their skills sharp.

♦ *Utilize vendor training.* If you distribute or resell anything, the people who made what you sell are great training resources. They should be extremely knowledgeable about what you sell for them; and they will have an opportunity to hear from your frontline salespeople about what the market thinks of their latest product innovation or price increase. It is also very important to have your people hear from someone other than yourself. When you have any outsider present, make sure that you are visible and present for the beginning and the end of the session. This shows that you support the presenter and the material and this increases the perception of value among your team. (You are always selling.) Bolting out the door is *not* recommended.

When you add training into your annual budget, you will, as a smart businessperson and manager, want to know what the return on investment will be. One of the best responses I received when I mentioned the return on investment that they could expect because of my sales training for their team was, "It is not an issue of what I get as an immediate return. The bottom line is, I can't afford *not* to train my people." This was music to my ears, and the person ended up hiring me to train his team. The issue stands, however: What is the return on investment?

Unfortunately, no one has created a matrix for this equation. There is no formula or guaranteed technique that proves that if I invest X dollars, I get Y dollars back in sales.

The true return on your investment must be measured in its context: The exact dollar return or increase is a direct and comforting measurement, but it need not be the only one used. The human issues (e.g., motivation, confidence, willingness, or ability to deal with defeat) also provide a return.

Training is an ongoing exercise, and if you do it once a year and never mention it again, you cannot expect your staff to take it seriously. Similarly, supervising your sales staff must be an ongoing commitment. An important lesson for a sales manager is, "You cannot expect what you do not inspect." While this caveat applies to the inspection of daily arrivals, as well as reporting of and generation of activity by your individual sellers, which is important, it is very different to expect folks to focus on training and development if you do not follow up.

When training salespeople, include the following information:

♦ *Corporate policies and procedures.* You do not want anyone offering a money-back guarantee if your policies do not support that.

♦ *Paper-and-form processing and management.* The salesperson who handles a complaint from a customer yet cannot find the customer's file forces you to face the customer without any backup, which makes you appear to be out of touch with what your salespeople do and say. Before you ask the question, here's an answer you may not like: *Yes,* you are expected to know what your folks are doing and saying, regardless of whether that expectation is realistic.

♦ *Commissions.* The amount of time the average sales manager spends discussing, investigating, correcting, and explaining commissions is too high for the folks at NASA to estimate—be prepared, be patient, and be professional. In this instance, the local translation is: Be firm and consistent.

♦ *Competitive information.* What your competitors do, how they market and present themselves, how pricing from firm to firm differs are all essential details which are probably changing often.

♦ *Corporate history.* Where did the current company come from, how was it started, and why has it been able to stay in business? How does it make its profit? Where does your company fit into the history of the industry?

♦ *Decorum.* Both in and out of the office.

♦ *Budget.* Travel allowances, expenses, and the like.

♦ *Association involvement and dues.* Industry associations, Toastmasters, and so on.

♦ *Advancement opportunities and prerequisites.*

♦ *Presentation skills.*

♦ *Cold-calling skills.*

♦ *Relationship development and management skills.*

♦ *Closing techniques.*

   —Closing questions.

   —Closing philosophies.

   —Why closing is so important.

   —Even more emphasis on closing.

♦ *How to move a sales conversation forward.*

♦ *How to interact with other departments.*

♦ *Activities and work required to close a sale* (e.g., taking an order, or initiating the receipt of a purchase order, job order, response to a request for proposal [RFP], or any other indication of true commitment of a prospect to become a customer).

I grew up on the north shore of Long Island. We were fortunate enough to have a pool in our expansive backyard and a boat that we would take to the marina on the weekends to tool around Huntington Harbor and the Long Island Sound. I mention this because when I think about effective approaches to training salespeople, I think of how I learned to pilot a speedboat.

One of the things I had to understand when controlling the boat, guiding it through the water, and maintaining control of it was the concept of *accelerate, coast*. Accelerate, coast allowed for reliable, safe maneuvering, and it was easy to learn.

I remember my time behind the wheel with more pleasure than my time swimming in the water, but when my father first allowed me to take the wheel of our 18-foot speedboat, I was nervous that I would do something wrong. Duck Harbor, one of the preferred places to take skiers back then, was a protected cove separated from the rough waters of the bay by a curved land mass, so the water was always "like glass."

When my father spoke about how to control this machine built for speed, I listened with great interest. Imagine a 15-year-old boy controlling a boat that could do 40 knots. Eventually, he told me I could start to drive the boat while one of my brothers water-skied. Before I could pull a skier, however, I had to develop a feel for how the boat would respond to different commands like accelerate, coast. I had to know where the other boats were headed and stay out of their way. I had to have my brother feel comfortable enough to know that I would not send him onto the land, into a rough wake, or into the bow of an oncoming cabin cruiser.

The parallel in training salespeople comes from the different ways in which I slowly earned the confidence and trust of my father and all the other boats with which we shared the water. In sales training, everyone gains confidence and skill at his or her own pace.

When I discuss classroom training, I like people to understand the different dynamics there. In training, we should also learn to accelerate, coast, accelerate, coast.

I like to offer a lot of information, give people time to digest it, ask them to test and apply it, and then test them on it. I like to ask specific detailed questions about what we have discussed and questions that are more emotional like: "So, how did it feel when you could apply that in a way that you were comfortable with?" "How did you feel when you realized it would work for you?"

Emotional questions always get people talking: Some people try to figure out what you want to hear, mentally deciding if they are going to be a yes-person. Other people try to figure out where you are going with your thinking, trying to second- or third-guess you. Then there are the folks who just want to learn, and these are the people with whom you get the most mileage. Emotional questions work well because they provide you with a guideline for when to accelerate and when to coast.

Another aspect to piloting the speedboat was the fact that a sudden stop was both difficult and uncomfortable. When you build up speed in a speedboat, you generate a wake—a wave of water. If you suddenly cut the power, the boat may stop moving, but the wave doesn't. Very often, the wake that followed the boat would follow it right to the stern and lift the rear of the boat. It was a bit unsettling.

Other times, the water would not be so subtle, and it would flow right into the boat, causing Dad to intone calmly, "Get the pump!" My brothers and I (or whoever was in the boat, *except* Dad) would have to pump and scoop the water out of the hold and get us seaworthy once again.

This backup or swell of water is what happens to your trainee if you expect too much, or if you don't find a balance between accelerate and coast. I learned quickly that all things were easier to manage if my speed increased or decreased gradually.

I am not known as the most patient man among my family or circle of friends, but I do appreciate the delicate balance that a small boat in the water must maintain. I equate that to a steady, progressive increase of proficiency, understanding, and effectiveness when training a professional salesperson.

Throughout this chapter, you hear from training veterans who provide you with great ideas and insights. But I wanted the analogy of piloting the boat and developing comfort doing so to be set in your mind. Patience is the order of the day, when boating and training. In addition, Training is about pacing, driving, letting someone try and possibly fail, learning, adapting, and adopting.

That's a long sentence, a long list, and a great way to approach training, in the classroom or individually. When you are working one on one, you really get to the fun and pleasure associated with training. It is both art and science. Art (in my opinion) is about intuition, creativity, and risk. Science is about observation and discovery.

Training is a true joy for me when the center of attention floats back and forth between the trainer and the trainee. When the trainee is applying a learned skill, the trainer is observing. When the trainer is demonstrating a skill or procedure, the trainee is observing. The joy is evident when the trainee applies the skill and observes how it affects her progress.

NEEDS ASSESSMENT

When you conduct a needs assessment, you have to look through a lens that starts with organizational objectives and ends with what will help this person make it as part of your team. I like asking people what training they would like to receive over a calendar year, and although suggestions are encouraged and welcomed, I am reluctant to have them choose the vendor. Your job is to create a balanced view, a balanced assessment, and a balanced delivery. Key word: balance. If your human resources (HR) department has various vendors trying to sell training to your company, ask if you can sit in on one or two of the presentations. (It can be not only a fun exercise to see how these salespeople sell but also a recruiting opportunity.) In addition, you get the cooperation of a department that is accustomed to being bombarded with demands, as opposed to help and suggestions. You have to get along with everyone in the organization, and when you have a candidate for an open position, your HR department can make you look great by helping to attract a good candidate.

Needs assessment is a balance between what you want your folks to improve on, what they think they should improve on, and accounting for your budget of time and funding. When you conduct or bring in training from the outside, it is all about time, commitment, and support. If you are not enthusiastic about it, your folks will not take it seriously.

Now, let's look at some other perspectives, some ideas about budgeting, and some ideas for you, The Ultimate Sales Manager, on how to train your people.

Thad Seligman has been involved in training salespeople for a large portion of his professional career. He has written and delivered a variety of programs and systems. During his tenure as training development manager for NAI Global (a commercial real estate service firm), he coordinated two "university" meetings per calendar year and brought people together from varied experience levels. He prepares, presents, and hires some training vendors to present key material at these events. We spoke about training and how it fits into the toolkit of The Ultimate Sales Manager. He subscribes to Attribute 8 of The Ultimate Sales Manager.

**Attribute 8: Always work to earn
the trust of your folks, one by one.**

Thad felt that managing and training were very closely related. He told me:

Salespeople say that they like the freedom of sales. They manage themselves and no one is looking over their shoulder; they either make enough money (or not) at the end of the year, and that is the perfect life for them.

The reality I have discovered in my 35 years of experience is that salespeople in their heart of hearts want to be managed. They want to be helped along the way. They want to be nurtured and cared for; they may not want you to hug them (figuratively) when you want to, but they want it when they want it. They may not agree with all of your philosophies and procedures; they might fight, kick, and scream the whole way, but the key is to manage a person so that he does not fight, kick, and scream. You need to be able to manage him in a way that he thinks suits his needs, instead of yours.

Thad Seligman tells us:

Salespeople want to have "hands on"—they want to be managed. They *do not* want to be told what to do. They want you to be a resource, a helper, a defender, and an advocate.

CLASSROOM TRAINING

You must create, maintain, and conduct a consistent classroom-type training schedule, outside of sales meetings and according to a scheduled agenda. You have to be an advocate of training at all times, and as such, you need to make sure that you have the ability to hold your teams' attention.

It is important to know who you want to attend and what you want them to learn. Planning training is similar to planning sales meetings—expect that you will probably never run through the exact same topics from one sales meeting to the next. You will, however (as you build your team and experience turnover), cover the same topics in many different training sessions.

Preparing for Classroom Training

Your preparation for the classroom experience must be detailed so that you stay on point. You will have enough of a challenge preventing your students from going off on irrelevant tangents—you have no leeway to do so.

In a classroom environment, I like to engage and involve the group as soon as possible, maintaining that involvement throughout. Over my years of speaking in front of groups, I have developed a few techniques that have served me well when I was presenting a commission change or conducting cold-calling training.

Step by step, let's walk through what you will do from the time you choose a topic through when you deliver the material:

Step 1: Make notes, over a day or two, about what you think will be the most relevant topics to discuss.

Step 2: Assemble these notes into an outline similar to a book report that you might have created in school. Talk about the impact, the goal, the structure, and the take-away points—what do you want people to "take away" from the training session?

Step 3: Review these notes a few times because each time you read them, you will probably change the delivery. You always want to have a payoff or key deliverable. I like to create language that will become part of what people say in the selling day.

Step 4: Once you have a set of notes that you are comfortable with, get up, walk around, and either silently or aloud, walk through the transitions from topic to topic, and create some key phrases that you will deliver verbatim during the session.

Step 5: Recording this walk-through is a very good idea. Listen to yourself discuss or explain the concepts or procedures. Do not be overly critical, but clean up weak transitions and unclear statements. Weave in a joke or a humorous cartoon about business or sales that will not offend anyone.

Step 6: Once you have done a walk-through, leave the notes and prepare your opening.

Step 7: Open each session by telling your folks the day's topic. Ask them what they would like to get out of a session specifically geared toward that topic.

Step 8: Write their responses on a flipchart or white board and keep those in plain sight.

Step 9: Now, you are ready for Toastmasters' rule of thumb:

♦ Tell them what you are going to tell them.
♦ Tell them.
♦ Tell them what you told them.

This means that you want to be clear about your topic. State it. Break it down over the course of the classroom time, via the notes you have prepared.

Step 10: Create a review that will sum up what you have presented, and then take it to the next level: Ask people to compare what you discussed to what was on their "expectations list." I like to leave their list of expectations hanging throughout the session because it keeps me on task, and I refer to it often. It also gives me a map of where I should direct the conversation or presentation. I open the session with "What would you like to get out of this training?" because it elicits involvement, feedback, and dialogue. The pressure is immediately off me, the presenter, and on the group to become a part of what is discussed. This is such a powerful technique that it has saved me many times from losing track of a topic, and most important, maintaining the interest and involvement of my audience.

An audience can be three people sitting around a conference table. It can be 500 people at your national sales meeting. Both groups deserve the respect you show for their time, by asking them to get involved without asking, "Who would like to participate?"

As I mentioned earlier, emotional questions are powerful, because they get your people talking. If you are conducting a class on negotiating a rate or margin on your product or service, you want to ask, "Where do you think negotiations can go off course with a new customer?" This gets a discussion going and develops some momentum and fuel for the delivery of your concepts.

Training salespeople is not easy, so do not fool yourself. They are always wondering who the smartest, wittiest, or quickest person in the room is. They are always thinking, "How is this going to make me more money?" You can even use that to entice them. When you ask what they would like to get out of this class, but no one says it, humbly ask, "Who here would like to make more money next month?" When the grins begin, and the hands begin to elevate themselves, write it down, and credit someone in the room—"I could see that on your face, Phil!"

Tips for Classroom Training

Classroom training should never go more than 75 minutes without a break. After each break, review what you have discussed: *Have the students tell you.*

Make it fun—offer goofy prizes to the person with the most right answers. If it is a large group, split them into teams. Have them compete against each other to come up with the longest, most accurate list.

After the review, build on your previous discussion, keeping them involved by asking questions that are more emotional:

- ◆ So, what do you think of this so far?
- ◆ How do you think this will work for you?
- ◆ How would you feel about delivering this on your next sales presentation?
- ◆ What do you think your current customers would think of this idea?

Emotional questions incorporate words like *think, want, hope, help,* or *believe.* These types of questions are powerful because no one answers these with a yes or a no. Everyone has an opinion. When you ask people to share their opinions, you learn how to sell, parent, lead, or manage better.

Keep in mind this bit of wisdom I have picked up over the years: You will never learn anything while you are talking.

At the end of the classroom session, ask them to walk through the expectations with you. If an expectation was not met, discuss why: Time? Tangents? Great discussions about how to apply a concept that you thought would take five minutes to discuss but in actuality had profound relevance to your folks?

Please make sure that you end earlier than you advertised. If the class is scheduled from 10:00 A.M. to 12 P.M., get people out of the room at 11:45 A.M.

All of these are valid and useful. All of these make you someone who can create a culture that looks forward to training. Early in my selling career, training was avoided like the plague because it was an exercise by the senior reps to talk down to the rookies—it was torture.

Classroom training is a risky business because you have to have all the answers. You have to engage people in discussion about what you teach, as opposed to delivering a sermon. It is not instruction or command—it is training.

When I was employed as the division sales trainer by SPI, a division of ICN Pharmaceuticals, I built a training manual, and every new hire worked through that manual from start to finish. It was the first time I had created a training agenda and course material, and it was a great step forward for me. (I still have a copy on my desk as I write this.) It was great to hear several years after I left the company that some of the salespeople still used that manual as a training tool. The manual was designed to standardize the training cycle of every person who worked in the department. The manual was required regardless of whether the person had been selling for 20 minutes or 20 years. When each person began working in that department, we built a schedule of classes, coaching, testing, and one-on-one work, beginning on the first day.

I like to think that this process contributed to the reduction in turnover that the department had suffered before we began, but a large part of the increase in retention of good people, as well as the increase in sales revenue, was attributable to my partner in the department—a very amiable, talented manager—Troy Moss.

Troy had a mild yet driven demeanor that always impressed me. I have a hard-charging personality, and my approach to training at that time was not that it was a high priority—it was the *only* priority. Troy helped me to maintain some perspective, and he was instrumental in my success at selling training to the staff.

When we took salespeople off the selling floor for training, all they thought about was how much money they were losing, and who on the floor might be calling on the leads to whom they had hoped to sell something that day.

We worked together very well because Troy worried about and dealt with absences, lateness, personality conflicts, and commission disputes. I dealt with classroom training and floor coaching. (I would prowl the selling floor, listening for opportunities to assist, suggest, and encourage. Troy made it clear to me early on that when I walked behind people as they sold on the phone, it made many of them feel as though they were being monitored or micromanaged.)

In the end, Troy and I built a team and a production level that was the best in our corporate history. We introduced intermittent cash spiffs for certain attainments or accomplishments on a particular day. We implemented several concepts and structures that I still teach today. We increased the revenue in that environment by dramatic multiples, and it all happened because we found a balance between our approaches, personalities, and responsibilities.

Aside from being consistent and comprehensive, training sessions must also be interactive, focused, and relevant. During several of the interviews conducted with the people you hear from in these pages, I was reminded of many admonitions, with one of the most common ones being: "Make sure that you do not waste your salespeople's time." In meetings, on sales calls, in training sessions, during coaching opportunities—no matter where the interaction might be—make sure that your people get something out of the time you have asked them to invest.

Thad Seligman's classroom experience is extensive. He says:

> Typically, an audience of 60 people is going to include people of all walks of life, with different personalities, different educational backgrounds, and you have to find a way to train each one differently because you will manage them differently.

TRAINING BEYOND THE CLASSROOM

Thad also believes:

> In addition to being committed to training, the sales manager must be well organized. The Ultimate Sales Manager, regardless of the function she is performing, is a coach, a monitor, a mentor, a babysitter, a leader, a trainer, an administrator, a strategist, a visionary, a disciplinarian, a protector of their salespeople, and a psychiatrist.

These point toward the power of Attribute 9 of The Ultimate Sales Manager.

**Attribute 9: Work first to understand,
before you expect to be understood.**

Thad continues:

> You have to have your couch, with a warm blanket and a glass of milk next to it. The salespeople see their role as straightforward, and as a result, they have a singular view: Go out, sell the product, and bring the money back. As managers, we must think along a more strategic path.

The Ultimate Sales Manager lives the formula:

$$Prepared + Professional = Productive$$

When thinking about training, there are budgetary considerations, and many of the people I spoke to in preparing this book suggested that 10 percent to 15 percent of gross revenue should be invested in training.

I use the word *invest* because when we say "spend" there is pain or discomfort associated with the mental image created. Then, there is the need to consider the amount of your time you invest in training. Thad says:

> If you include focused training sessions, including one-on-one counseling, where you might be working with a salesperson individually, based on a particular sales situation, I find that 50 percent of my time is dedicated to or related to training.
>
> As a budget item, we estimate15 percent to 20 percent of the gross (in Commercial Real Estate it is smaller), when managing 35 to 40 people, so we spend $50,000 to $60,000.
>
> Training for salespeople is one of the most important budget items and should be done on an ongoing basis. Other professions have continuing education. Why do salespeople need ongoing training from the direct sales manager? Because salespeople are convinced that they do not need training.
>
> A salesperson having the best year of her life is exciting, but the real question when you think about it is: This may be your best year, but compared to what?

The Ultimate Sales Manager is constantly balancing the enjoyment of an employee's performance and thinking about how much more the person *could* do. When I was a manager, I developed an ability to tell what was getting in the way of someone getting to the next level. For some, the next level could be making their quota for the first time; for others, it could mean quantum leaps in their income in the short term.

One of the points that many people I interviewed in preparation for this book agreed on wholeheartedly was that most salespeople don't realize how talented they are and how much potential they have. This is a frustration for the managers, but a point of opportunity for them as well.

Thad continues:

There is another fun path to pursue when training: making sales-people better-rounded. I did a 12-week self-hypnosis training program. Half of the salespeople who went through it embraced it, and among that group, we saw a 28 percent increase in their sales productivity.

I am not sure if the program was the reason or if they were all naturally moving up. I could, however, tell that they were better prepared, they were calmer, their minds were sharper, clearer, and they had gotten good rest the night before.

At that point, I asked myself: "How do you measure the technical skills or life-skill training?"

The question is, "Can I put too much emphasis on training?" And my answer is: No.

Training Options

You have many options for how you will conduct training, with the most popular being:

- ◆ Classroom
- ◆ Video
- ◆ Audio
- ◆ Books (see recommended sales books on our web site at www.salesmanagerguide.com)
- ◆ Computer-based training (see the list of recommended vendors at www.salesmanagerguide.com)

Training ranges across a wide spectrum. It happens in the classroom, as well as in the car on the way to or from an appointment. It happens standing at someone's desk, and it happens when you react or respond to a salesperson's actions, attitude, and performance.

Salespeople traditionally invest very little money or time in their own professional development. You cannot fold your arms in dissatisfaction and say, "Why don't they invest in themselves? They *should."* The problem is that what *should* be and what *is* are often two different things in real life.

Do not drive a wedge between you and your team members by assuming or thinking that they should do something with which they do not agree. Offer opportunities. Make options available. Make the investment. Wait and see what happens.

Since you will never know if people are going to stay on board, or if they are going to perform for you over time, the optimistic view is the only one that will allow you to maintain your own mental health.

DEVELOPMENT

Development is a close cousin to training, or they might actually be twins, because many of the sales managers I spoke with had significant trouble distinguishing between the two. Training is often seen as an "I teach, you learn" interaction. Training can go on during a drive to a sales appointment or over lunch. But development is distinguishable in that it is more personalized. It encompasses the whole body of the personality, circumstances, and challenges of the individual.

My daughter pointed out a great quote to me while we were filling out college applications for her. Her high school coordinated a trip to Europe for a group of select students this past year, and she had the opportunity to visit Rome. After seeing Michelangelo's *David*, she was told of Michelangelo's famous quote:

There are masterpieces hidden within the rock. It is my job to pull them out.

Are your salespeople actually masterpieces hidden in a piece of marble, waiting to be developed? I hope so, and I hope that you believe it to be true.

◆

Bob Dean is an executive vice president and managing director with Grubb & Ellis Company in Sacramento, California. He has held Sales Management positions at various levels for over 30 years. He gets up every morning to go to work managing salespeople. I asked him: "Who in their right mind would want to be a sales manager?" He laughed, and told me:

> I have asked myself that for 30 years. Each New Year I make a commitment to myself that if I stop enjoying it, I will stop doing it. For over 30 years of my life, I have woken up every morning full of energy. Sales management is not for everyone. You must enjoy it, be energized by it, and be used to the hurdles and heartaches.

Bob and I spoke at length about a variety of issues, and his insights on how he develops people really resonated with me. Bob is a true professional. He has a productive, prepared staff that, as a group, is highly productive. His team enjoys a tremendous environment. The experiences I have had when visiting his office have stayed with me, because I have always walked out thinking: "That's how you run a sales team." Bob says:

> I am a subscriber to Ken Blanchard's concept of situational leadership. You get more out of people if you manage and respond to them based on their level of experience, skill set, knowledge base, and attitude. These make up what I call an individual's professional maturity. Based on where they are, with a specific task or assignment, you will get more out of them because they will be more motivated via different approaches from directive and supportive to leaving them alone.
>
> I have effectively used situational leadership since 1976. With new employees, I will spend a lot of time with them. We talk often, and I make sure that they know my parameters. In fairness, and to develop them properly, I must make sure that they know my expectations very clearly. They double-check with me on a lot of things. They know where I stand, and they know where the

company stands. This increases their ability to operate with confidence and be more motivated. I don't want them too comfortable, however.

If they are new salespeople, my approach is to meet with them first thing in the morning, tell them what the goals are and what I expect for the day. Let's say that I want them to make 10 cold calls and then come and see me. This is good, because they know what is expected of them.

I will closely inspect what I expect and continue that as we go along. I have four tenets:

1. Directing
2. Coaching
3. Supporting
4. Delegating

As far as being professionally mature, I don't assume that their eight years in another organization is the same as eight years with us.

Professional maturity speaks to the fact that you cannot expect people to know the history and culture of your company from day one. So, if they don't, they are not professionally mature, as far as the company history is concerned. I would have them understand that as they work up the professional maturity curve, I will fall back, inspect less often, have interactions less often, and have expectations and reviews less often. It is a straight-line continuum. The higher the level of professional maturity, the lower the need for:

♦ Inspection
♦ Direction
♦ Task Orientation

New hires require different inspection and direction than someone who has been with us for some time. Here is what I explain and expect from new hires:

♦ The sales job is difficult—it pays well for good performance.
♦ Every salesperson likes to do certain things, but there are other things he prefers not to do. Concentrate your attention on the things you don't like to do—because your competition is doing those things.

◆ It sounds odd, but I tell new hires: "If you feel really good at the end of the day at any time during your first year, you are doing something wrong."

Paranoia and discomfort are the keys to success, because I want them looking over their shoulder, assuming that someone is coming up after them. Discomfort may not sound like fun, but it is required for someone to be able to grow.

Salespeople should be on the phone by the second day. They do not have to know everything about the product or the service before being ready to call.

The best phrase you can deliver is: "That's a great question. Let me get the details on that for you. When can I call you?"

Bob and I spoke about this at length. The Ultimate Sales Manager makes sure that new hires get their feet wet quickly. The longer you avoid or delay getting people on the phone, or out in front of prospects and customers, the harder it will be for them to get into a rhythm. Sales is not for the weak of heart. It is intimidating, and that is why it pays so well. Get your new folks out in front of prospects within the first week of employment.

YOU ESTABLISH THE ENVIRONMENT

There is an old saying that every individual contributes to the relationships that he is in. The environment that you create and maintain as a sales manager is highly dependent on you. Every time you walk by someone's desk, he or she wonders what you are thinking. People are not paranoid—they are just aware.

The environment must be established with humor, energy, verve, confidence, and professionalism. As I mentioned earlier, the environment in Bob Dean's office is one of the best (fun, professional, and productive) that I have ever visited as an outsider.

The environments I have created in my past management positions always aspired to that exact feeling. Everyone who walks in should understand what is going on there, from prospective new employees to vendors and, most important, customers.

Bob continues:

> Most important, I want a distinct, tangible environment. Here are the conscious decisions I think The Ultimate Sales Manager makes:
>
> ♦ Hire (and keep) people who are team players, who want to get along with one another, and who are part of a culture of people who actually enjoy being around each other.
> ♦ We work hard, and we have a lot of fun.
> ♦ Fun is the overriding criteria.
> ♦ A 100-percent-commission sales environment *could* have people who tend to be self-centered. There must be a clear message that there should not be any jealousy when someone wins something. We are looking for a very positive reputation in our industry and community.
>
> I enjoy the fact that people who work for us make a decent living. There is not an air of jealousy that someone makes a good living. The success of anyone in the office is helpful for the overall reputation of the office. If I could not hire people I enjoy, I would wake up January 1 and decide not to work here anymore. Your standards and actions become the new company standard. Whether you raise or lower the standard is up to you.

Bob goes on to say:

> I am aware of my pace, both physical and verbal. I rarely walk anywhere slowly. That sets a pace. My pace is picked up in the bullpen, and it is reflected. People adopt it.
>
> You are always being watched and listened to: You may use a simple phrase during a sales call with one of your folks, and then you go on a call with them a few weeks later, and you hear that same phrase. It's satisfying to know that you are being listened to. It's hard to miss, actually. Don't ever think that your folks are not paying attention—they are *always* paying attention.
>
> Your energy level is responded to, as well. I have been nicknamed "the Energizer Bunny." It bothered me at first, but now I am

thrilled because it means that at this stage of my life, I still have energy and passion for what I do.

Bob is the inspiration and the embodiment of Attributes 10 and 11 of The Ultimate Sales Manager.

Attribute 10: Establish and maintain an environment of trust, hard work, fun, enthusiasm, and confidence.

Attribute 11: Lead with the intent to elevate the team.

Development is a precursor to leadership. You cannot lead people with simply a title or a mandate. Being a good leader means being charismatic. It means fine-tuning your approach for each person. Training facilitates your opportunity to develop people. By helping people reach greater heights, you position yourself as a leader. You must respect the trust and confidence that is invested in you when people choose to follow you. This allows you to position yourself and operate as their coach.

Okay, Coach—Where Is Your Whistle?

Coaching allows us to personalize training when the topics are solely focused on how each skill, procedure, and task is handled and managed by the trainee. The feedback, interaction, debate, and encouragement bind the two people in a profound way. Coaching is ongoing, personal, and powerful.

The best advice I ever received about coaching came from a Hall of Fame NFL coach whom I had the good fortune to sit next to on an airplane. I was traveling first-class from a seminar in Richmond, Virginia, and had to switch planes in Chicago. As I approached the gate, I noticed a short man with gray hair. I had the feeling that I recognized him, but I could not place him. I boarded the plane, and found that the man was putting his things down in the seat next to mine. When he said hello and I heard his voice, I knew immediately that he was Marv Levy, the legendary coach of the Buffalo Bills. Many years prior to our meeting, he had taken his team to the Super Bowl four years in a row.

As we traveled, I struck up a casual conversation with him (not wanting to sound like or appear to be an overeager fan). We talked about the menu and the distance of the flight, and then he asked me why I was traveling. I told him about my sales-training career, and he was polite, interested, and gracious.

We landed, and said our good byes.

Here's where the story gets interesting.

Four months later, on a flight from Los Angeles to Chicago, the coach sat next to me—*again*. I could not believe it. After a few minutes, we started talking again, and I reminded him of our last "trip together." He seemed to remember me, and we talked about football and other things. After a while, he asked me what I was going to do in Chicago. I explained that I had been hired to speak before a management team of a major hotel chain about coaching (of all things).

I then steeled up my nerve and asked Mr. Levy: "What are the three keys to being a great coach?" Here's what he told me:

♦ You have to know the Xs and Os better than anyone. Know all the assignments and responsibilities of everyone on the team.

♦ You have to get along with everyone in the organization, top to bottom.

♦ You *never* make a promise on which you cannot personally deliver. (Never guarantee a starting position to a rookie—or anyone else you are trying to recruit. Tell them that the starting right guard position is open, and you would love to have them come and compete for it.)

This is great advice from a great coach, and it is especially fitting for The Ultimate Sales Manager. These three simple admonitions can guide all aspects of what you do, and really set your team down the right path.

Coach Levy was sincere and passionate about what he said, and I believed that he lived by these simple rules. His players loved playing for him. The media loved him because he was a no-nonsense guy, and the front office obviously loved and respected him because as of the time of this writing, he has just been drawn out of retirement to run the football operations for his old team.

Know the Xs and Os. Get along with everyone (not like them, or have them like you—*get along*). *Never* promise what you cannot personally deliver.

When you coach your folks, you are taking training to a personal level. You are providing a protected environment for people to vent or reveal their personal doubts and for you to offer some encouragement outside of bonuses and other incentives. Time is the commodity that all of your people are going to want of you more than anything else.

Backfilling Your Position

Eighty percent of sales managers have come from the sales ranks, and they are probably *not* the top-performing salespeople.

In order for you to advance, you must identify and groom someone to be your replacement.

Attribute 12: Spend time looking for a suitable replacement for yourself.

If someone is a consistently producing salesperson (regardless of how highly she ranks), if this person is consistently adding to the bottom line (and is not a drag on the team or division), but fits into the bread-and-butter segment of a sales team (see Chapter 5), this person is probably a strong candidate for sales management.

Having made a living selling prepares you for sales management because you have fought the fight and learned how to *win* the fight (and you can mentor other people from personal experience, validated by you being able to say: "Yes, I have made a cold call and been shot down. Yes, I did have to pay back a commission. Yes I have gone an entire month without closing a deal, and I have considered applying for a Civil Service Job.") Effective sales managers must have experienced these essential trials to have people follow them.

Leadership is a broad and important topic. One aspect of your job as a leader is to be able to evaluate performance and to communicate with each individual what he or she is doing well, what he or she needs to improve on, and what role he or she plays on your team. This is covered in Chapter 3.

Let's end this chapter with Attribute 13 of The Ultimate Sales Manager.

Attribute 13: Understand that your job is about leadership, solving problems, and taking responsibility.

3

PERFORMANCE EVALUATION

Since the sales profession is overwhelmingly perceived as being a numbers game, let's talk about numbers. Many sources detail how many people you will have to hire and train before you can start to establish a credible, reliable team, or how many cold calls a salesperson must make before getting a meeting, proposal, presentation, or deal. Such numbers are great. I love numbers because they are clean, reliable, and they simply do not lie.

Every time I have considered changing someone's professional life (letting him go, releasing him, sending him on his way—whichever euphemism you are comfortable with for firing someone), the first thing I looked at was his or her numbers: gross profit, total sales dollars, percentage of attainment of goal, and so on. And the simple "math" throughout this book is this formula:

Preparation + Professionalism = Productivity

But when you evaluate the performance of your folks, you must ensure that you evaluate them on their own merits, their own history and tendencies, and (as far as you can see) their own potential.

Writing an evaluation is a difficult task because in order to be effective, the individual administering the review must conduct the evaluation so that the person being evaluated takes away the appropriate message. However, people will interpret different messages from the same type of evaluation. I find this fascinating.

Some will look at the ranking you give them compared to their peers. Others will ignore that and only be concerned with whether you recommend them for the next promotion (say, from local accounts to regional or national), leading a team, or possibly (oddly enough) even the next management position. Still others will dismiss the evaluation process altogether.

Maire O'Dwyer Houston is a sales director who leads the staffing division for Yahoo Hotjobs. She and her team sell to some of the other individuals who contributed their stories to this book. It is a small world, and one that is much more fun when we get to work with (and sell to) people whom we respect and enjoy. Maire and I have had several conversations about sales management, and she was very anxious to share some of her experiences and ideas with you.

Evaluating the performance of salespeople is a detailed, tricky business. Top performers make themselves known in a variety of ways, but where do we get the future top performers? What do we look for when we are deciding who should have more responsibility and larger accounts or be promoted within the division or team?

Maire is a seven-year management veteran who started in sales herself. She sold and served as a sales manager with Hotjobs prior to the company being acquired by Yahoo. In preparation for this book, we had a great conversation about the hows and whys of performance evaluation. She really opened my eyes to the fact that the power of good performance evaluation is an ongoing exercise, and it is woven into the fabric of your daily interactions with each individual on your team.

Writing evaluations may be tedious, but many HR departments require them. Evaluations may have to be completed at night or on the weekends, but they are necessary documents of an ongoing conversation.

Our themes throughout this book are (1) vision precedes everything, (2) the three-P formula (Prepared + Professional = Productive), and (3) the definition of "to manage": *to get the most out of*. Maire's
refreshing insights about these follow:

> Salespeople are measured by the numbers, but there is more to the
> picture. I think before you can start with the performance evalua-
> tion, you have to start with the goals and expectations you set for
> people. I feel that this is what attracts many people to sales: The
> numbers speak for themselves.
>
> You are measured in comparison to your peers, and it is easy to
> see who is number one and number two. It doesn't matter who
> happens to be the first person in the office, or the last person in
> the office, or who makes a good impression on the boss when the
> boss comes to town for a week. Even though I think that most of
> the time, it may be the first person in, the last person out may also
> be the top performer; all this is only part of the equation. Num-
> bers in and of themselves are not the only thing you are looking
> for in the well-rounded salesperson.
>
> You are looking for people with all-around professionalism, who
> are looking to take the steps to improve as a salesperson because
> that is always possible in sales. There is no perfect salesperson.
> There is not anyone who cannot learn something new about the
> profession. For junior salespeople, you want to determine the steps
> to get to those numbers. To say that you want $100 thousand in
> sales per quarter is meaningless to someone who has only been on
> the job for a couple of months. You need to outline the steps that
> need to be taken to be successful, like: "Find this many leads, make
> this number of phone calls, find this number of prospects, go on
> this many appointments, and submit this many proposals."
>
> Give them an indication of the daily tasks and steps that it will
> take to have them get there. Once they have mastered the sales
> basics, it is important to emphasize that hitting these numbers is
> only part of the equation. If you want to be a top performer, you
> have to be someone who will contribute to the team; someone
> with the potential to move up in the organization (especially if it
> is a growing organization, like ours). You want people who have

the potential to take on bigger accounts, not just someone who can hit numerical goals.

JK: I hear consistent comments are about growth and advancement.

MOH: It is very rare that you find many people in sales who envision themselves cold-calling until retirement. If you communicate that you are looking for people that want to move up in the organization, the way that you set goals and measure performance needs to reflect that. This does include (yet goes beyond) mere attainment of a goal.

When you consistently bring into the equation that this person hits his numbers (that should be a baseline measurement—in sales, you have to hit the goals that we set forth), then you give people an idea of how they can get to the next level.

JK: So, you are always evaluating the individuals on your team?

MOH: Yes. I want people who will add to the team, build their sales knowledge, assist with some of the management objectives, and help to identify better sales processes. I also look for other ways to pitch clients. As a manager, all of these are things that you track and recognize as being important. Recognizing that some people have done well, and that others may not have done these things, makes it easier to recognize those who should be promoted—the individuals who are offered the opportunity to work on special projects, who are called on to take on additional responsibility, who are given higher level prospects and clients to work on. You must be sure to recognize the attributes that you are looking for.

It all factors into how you, as a manager, set the tone: *"Just because you hit the numbers, does not mean that you will be promoted."* It will not be based on that alone. It's also important to recognize that you may have people who can hit numbers, or exceed them, but otherwise do not add value to the team. Making the numbers does not mean that you have secured your spot on the team. Adding numbers is

important, but if the salesperson is not adding value beyond that, there are fewer reasons to retain that person
over the long term.

Adding value, making the numbers, contributing to the
team—these are the things that we expect. This is what
helps us to create an environment where we have professional teams and professional team members.

There are a lot of sales opportunities out there where
someone using the phone to sell all day might be seen simply as a telemarketer, but when you create the right environment and hold people to high standards, you attract the best
of the best. People who want to work for a company like
Yahoo! make a significant income working in a professional
selling environment and essentially run their own business.

JK: Okay, do consistent approaches to expectations and performance evaluations help you recruit or promote?

MOH: I think that when you are part of the management
team, you need to see the people who bring in the revenue
as those that should have the opportunity for advancement,
and you can raise the stature of the job by setting a tone of
professionalism. If you want to do that, you need to make
sure that it is an environment where you are attracting individuals who meet those standards. If you do not, you are
not going to accomplish that goal. If you don't, you are not
going to attract people who you can promote to management, higher-level sales roles, or even other jobs entirely. If
you are in a growing organization, and you do not set that
standard, you will not be able to home-grow talent who
could make it to the managerial or executive level. We want
to make sure that we have a pool of talent to get us there. A
high percentage of Fortune 500 CEO's have started in
sales. We certainly want to create that type of environment.

SETTING EXPECTATIONS

As we continued our discussion, it struck me that Maire and her
team practice Attribute 14 of The Ultimate Sales Manager.

Attribute 14: Have a long memory
for people's accomplishments and a
short memory for their transgressions.

The Ultimate Sales Manager is in constant communication with her team to avoid some folks testing the "discipline" or "policy" envelope. Maire believes that success comes from consistent communication with her people.

JK: How often are you communicating what you expect of people?

MOH: That is an ongoing conversation. We are looking for an individual who can contribute on a lot of different levels. You need to make sure that, as a sales manager, you are not just measuring people on a spreadsheet. You are not sorting them as "most revenue" and using that as the key measurement for every occasion. It is important to recognize those people, but you have to recognize what their contributions are beyond that.

When building a sales organization, you need to make sure that you balance hitting the numbers and contributing at other levels. You do not set the tone only at quarterly or annual kick-off meetings. You set the tone by your day-to-day interactions with your people. This particularly applies if you are in an open environment, where you, the manager, might be more visible. The manager has to walk the walk, and talk the talk.

I think that what people find refreshing about sales is that you should always know where you stand in the eyes of your manager. Annual evaluations where you tell someone something that she has never heard before tend not to be effective with salespeople. I think that is why people are attracted to sales. We get people that work hard. If they work hard, have ambition, and want to be successful, they want the recognition and to know where they stand. They want to know how they can do better and where they are excelling or are falling short. You are in a great position, as a manager, to be able to have ongoing conversations and to make all that very clear.

I think that the clear indicators might be more difficult to define in nonsales management positions. There are not as many hang-ups in sales. Salespeople expect to hear feedback that will get them where they want to be and understand that they are going to be measured on many levels.

JK: So, what about recognition?

MOH: I think it is important to recognize salespeople in front of their peers and since the numbers are pretty well publicized in most sales organizations, I think the next level is to know some detail about your people. We go on sales trips twice a year, where I recognize the top performers in an awards ceremony. I may not know the individuals as well as their direct supervisor would, so for the first few days on the trip, I make sure to speak with them, their spouses, their manager, so I can share things about them that are relevant when I speak in front of a broader group of their peers. I want to recognize them and not just say, "This person is number one." because everyone already knows that—that's why they are on the trip. I want to articulate to that person's peers and managers how he or she got to that position.

Not only will I mention specific deals or what she does and how she goes about her day but also how she goes above and beyond. I think it makes that person feel good, and it shows others what it takes to be successful.

JK: How much time do you spend talking with your managers about managing salespeople?

MOH: We try to communicate, not commiserate. About 50 percent of our weekly conference call is spent on people management. We recently assigned smaller groups of salespeople to our managers, and we are very happy with how it has allowed us to give our managers the opportunity to get to know their people better. It also gives us the opportunity to have detailed discussions about those individuals, and it allows us to make sure that we are having very good communication.

KEY GUIDELINES

Maire says that there are key guidelines that The Ultimate Sales Manager needs to follow:

- ◆ Be consistent (you are asking salespeople to follow through—you need to be the master of the art).
- ◆ Understand that "the biggest deal of the day" may not be a huge deal for *you*, but it is a *very* big deal for the salesperson involved.
- ◆ Deal with issues as they come up, as opposed to allowing them to become larger issues down the road.
- ◆ Everyone has different levels of skill and motivation, so it is difficult to have effective communication unless it is one on one. Having smaller teams allows our managers to communicate effectively.
- ◆ Salespeople are, by nature, going to ask, "What's in it for me?"
- ◆ By having more one-on-one opportunity, you get to the ultimate "to manage" goal, getting the most out of your people.

During the time I have known and spoken with Maire, she has demonstrated Attribute 15 of The Ultimate Sales Manager.

Attribute 15: Maintain the skill and aplomb to get your salespeople to go where you want them to go—and have them think they took you there.

The Ultimate Sales Manager is an energetic, creative leader who is a great communicator.

I asked Maire: "Who in their right mind would want to go to work every day and manage salespeople?"

MOH: Someone who has become addicted to what I have become addicted to: winning and developing others into winners. It is refreshing in so many ways. You can have very real conversations with people about their professional and personal goals and ambitions.

Seeing people progress is a daily experience, as well as a long-term one. I have watched people come from every walk of life; all backgrounds come together in sales and succeed. We look for people with a work ethic, ambition, and who are not too afraid to fail because these people can succeed in sales in our environment. When they do succeed, it is such a gratifying experience.

I have always enjoyed the way the sales manager's success is truly dependent on the success of his or her team. It is very rare, in professional life, where your measurement as a manager is as clear-cut as it is in sales. We are a revenue-generating business unit.

The success of the salesperson contributes to the success of the manager, which contributes to the success of the sales director, and this accountability brings out the best in people. This is what gets people to commit, to be able to develop and participate. It is not for everyone.

SOME SPECIFICS

JK: Great stuff. Give me four words that define The Ultimate
      Sales Manager.
MOH: Communicator. Leader. Creative. Energetic.

Maire is very specific, and her team is made up of a bunch of sharp, hardworking folks. I know, because I have met, spoken with, and trained many of them.

Going forward, we look at a broad scope of issues pertaining to performance evaluation. Your next steps must be predicated by answering these few questions:

- ♦ What are the benchmarks for a salesperson on your team?
- ♦ Your organization has to have a few numbers for you, such as:
  —Cost of acquisition (e.g., cost to bring in a client or customer).
  —Cost of the sales desk (e.g., total dollars attributed and allotted to staffing a desk, from salary and benefits to office supplies and phone bills).
  —Gross profit necessary to cover these costs.

—Cost of delivery of your product or service (e.g., selling, delivering, and getting paid for your Gigabats).

When you look at each reporting period, and each salesperson, you will start to get a sense of where they fit into your overall scheme. This is where you start thinking about the intangibles each person demonstrates or offers. You may have some very talented people, yet they may not offer or provide those talents to the team, to your cause, or to you when you need them. After all, you are working with people. People are moody, people have other concerns besides the objectives you want them to focus on, and they have pressures beyond the numbers discussed previously.

Add to all of those ideas the fact that you, The Ultimate Sales Manager, are dealing not just with people and numbers but with *sales*people (who may be emotional, competitive, creative, or difficult to pin down), and you understand why taking on the responsibility of being a sales manager at any level is a Herculean effort. Take a brief moment to pat yourself on the back for doing something so amazing. But just a brief moment! Moving on, in Chapter 4, you learn about the Three-Tiered Sales Team™, which is a reliable approach to determining where every person on your team fits today, where he or she might fit tomorrow, and how you, The Ultimate Sales Manager, will lead your team.

4

THE THREE-TIERED SALES TEAM

One of my former bosses, and one of the smartest people I have ever met, Orestes Baez (OB, as almost everyone except his mom calls him), is now president of *The Flyer*, a weekly consumer advertising magazine in Tampa, Florida. An MBA from Clemson University, OB has that rare combination of academic accomplishment and real-world experience, making his one of the top minds in the country regarding sales management.

During my tenure as a sales manager reporting to OB (at the time, we both worked for the *Pennysaver*, a sister publication to *The Flyer*, in Southern California. He was the regional manager and had 12 managers and over 150 salespeople reporting to him). I ran a team of specialists who sold advertising solutions and programs to two specific vertical markets: real estate and employment. This meant that some of the folks reporting to me sold ads to real estate agents, leasing companies, and housing developers, while others sold to employers, employment agencies, and the like.

I was hired by OB at a point in my career when I had about 12 years of selling experience and 7 years of sales management experience.

I interviewed OB recently in preparation for this chapter and asked him the question I asked all the great experts whom you hear from in these pages: "Who in their right mind would want to go to work every day and manage salespeople?"

I ask this tongue in cheek, but I also ask it to help define people like you and me. After a healthy laugh, OB gave me the best answer. He responded:

> People who want to win. You do not want to manage salespeople if you don't want to win. Every day you get passionate and reenergized. When you see the looks on the faces of salespeople, and the outcome of what they do as a result of your interactions, it is a great feeling. These feelings come from moments in time—opportunities, training, situations, customer calls—where the stuff that you have talked about comes together for the salesperson and for the customer. That is a *magical* moment, and I think that is why they want to manage salespeople. It is an evolving process that is extremely fluid, and as it changes, you have to adjust. The environment you sell in changes, and you have to adapt to that as well.

I took the opportunity to ask him another of the common questions I asked everyone I interviewed for this book: "In your opinion, how important is it for a sales manager to personally have selling experience?"

OB responded:

> It is critical that a sales manager have personal selling experience. While I have long believed that the greatest salespeople did not make the greatest sales managers because they do not have patience for the process, if you have *not* had sales experience, it is really hard to have credibility as a sales manager.

Of all the people interviewed in preparation for this book, only one felt that it was *not* critical for a sales manager to actually have done the work. I, personally, feel that sales is a profession that must be experienced to be truly understood and appreciated. There is only one thing in life that can teach you what it feels like to cold-call for three weeks: Cold-calling for three weeks.

After I accepted the position at the *Pennysaver*, OB walked me through a three-tiered way of looking objectively at the members of my team, which I am proud to say I have shared with many clients to great effect. The Ultimate Sales Manager uses this three-tiered approach to evaluate objectively the contribution that a particular salesperson makes or the headache that he or she creates. I agree with Maire O'Dwyer Houston's assertion: Your assessment and opinion of your salespeople *cannot* be limited to the numbers they produce. The reason: If generation of revenue is your only criteria, you may deal with the potential of allowing a de facto leader to influence the rest of your team.

Any and all organizations or assemblages of humans will have a "named" leader as well as a "de facto" leader. The de facto leader is the person whom others look to when you make an announcement, or issue a decree, to see if this person is on board with the edict or not. Depending on how you handle this person, you can either have an ongoing battle for leadership of the group, or you can have someone to help you when you need missions carried out. The de facto leader cannot become too much of a confidant for you (or vice versa) because this crosses the line of leadership and authority.

Ultimate Sales Managers are cautious, sell vision, and communicate. Listening to their people, they look for where they can help increase sales and balance lives, and where they should simply stay out of the way and allow people to do their jobs. The de facto leader will offer insight into the team as well as inroads into their heads and hearts.

When you think about the team or group you lead in three tiers, you immediately recognize that not everyone is going to be at the top of the leader board all the time.

IDENTIFYING THE THREE TIERS

OB says:

> A 15-person sales force is not made up of 15 top performers. In every environment, you have the top performers, the middle performers, and the low performers. Each tier has behavior—a propensity to say and do things in a certain way—that defines it.

Top performers are usually easiest to define. What does your organization perceive to be an indicator of the best sales perform-ance? Typically, what identifies a salesperson as a top performer? It is not the claim of being a top performer, it is her doing, being, and showing on paper that she is a top performer. Top performers are typically high maintenance and the go-to people. Even though they are high maintenance, they are the one in the selling conversation that knows how to get through the system and get to different types of customers. They are regularly successful in their ability to attract and maintain business. They are the upper echelon—the best of the best.

The other group that is easy to identify is the bottom tier. These are the people who met all the criteria you set when you hired them. They did all the things they were supposed to do. They went through all the training, and there has been coaching. Now that it is time to put the rubber on the road and they have had plenty of opportunity, they have just not connected the dots in a way that you can say on paper, "Gosh, you're really doing a good job!"

JK: So, what shows up on paper is really the test?

OB: We all grew up with report cards. In the sales environ-ment, it is not about whether you are a nice person, or a likeable person, it's about whether you are a person who provides the results that your organization needs to say, "Congratulations, you did a good job today."

If you are a person who is great at selling widgets, but your company wants and needs you to sell Gigabats, it is going to say to you, "Your value to us is in how many Giga-bats you sell, and you are not selling any."

The lower level is not the people you would not hire, it is the people who have made it through the gauntlet of your hiring process, and for whom you had great hopes, but they are just not meeting your expectations.

The largest percentages of individuals are those who fall in the middle. Those are your steady eddies, your plough horses, the people who, week in and week out, you can count on. They do what they need to do to get the job done. They require attention, but not as much attention as the top performers, and probably less attention than the bottom performers. They still need touches and direction but understand their job very clearly: They understand what's expected of them, how they are being measured, and how they get paid. They understand the product and their customers. They are not the greatest of the great but during some selling periods, they perform at a level where you can say, "Wow, that's awesome." They go through other periods where they are just average.

So, as a manager, because I was geographically spread out and managing a large sales force, I had to coach managers on how to maximize their time. I came from an environment that had a five-day close cycle. There was no extra time. You had to maximize the efforts of the salespeople. You had to figure out a way to get efficient and smart.

OB went on to explain to me that he was initially a bit taken aback by the short selling cycle. It was not only tight—it was carved in stone. The product had to go out on Monday to be in mailboxes by Wednesday, because that was the guarantee offered the paying advertisers. That tight schedule made him sit down and figure out a reliable way to assess and lead this group:

JK: So, how do you figure out how to divide your time as a manager?

OB: You go to your top performers, and you shake their hand, give them lots of accolades, and ask what obstacles you can remove.

With the middle people, the conversation is more about you asking, "How are you? What's going on? What are you facing that I can help with? Where are you struggling? Who should I go see with you? What do you need from me?" These people are very coachable. At the very least, you do not want them to get any worse, and at the very best, you are trying to get them to be in the upper middle tier, or trying to get them to move into the top tier.

The third tier tends to be where you spend time, offer direction, hold them accountable, and make sure that you have given them the appropriate time and effort, so that they have an opportunity to be successful. Then you hope that they move into the middle tier. If they do not move into the middle tier, you have to move them out of the organization and replace them with someone else.

Because this bottom tier requires so much time, you end up spending more time with the people not getting the job done, trying to help them get the job done, and you spend less time with the people who are getting the job done, and as a result, you risk your long-term performance.

The Ultimate Sales Manager always knows where she is going, and that means moving well from counseling to encouraging, from directing to leading, from cheering to correcting. OB continues:

The bottom tier starts to get "noisy" when they feel the pressure of performance and if they feel that the performance is going to determine whether they have a job. As sales managers, we tend to migrate toward people who make a lot of noise. The thought process is, "If I pay attention to them, will they stop making noise? God, I hope so."

Instead, you get sucked into spending your time with that bottom tier, which ends up costing you time with the top tier.

JK: So, ultimately, the sales manager's job is *not* done at his or her desk.

OB: No way. The metrics, the measurements—they are strictly a starting point for the sales manager. You use that information to identify where your opportunities lie. During the course of a selling cycle, you are using your high achievers to make sure that the critical, large customers are getting what they need, and the critical reps are getting what they need. If you are smart, you walk away from that by identifying what is portable. You use those conversations as a caveat for new ideas and new opportunities.

When speaking with the middle performers, you ask, "Have you tried what this other person is doing?" Or you can share some wrinkles that other salespeople are adding, and ask: "Can you add that?"

The most coachable people are looking to you for things that will help them, and are open to, even looking forward to, hearing what other successful people in their organization are doing.

The third tier puts you in a position to ask, "Are you in the right job? Do you really want to be here?" When you recount to them what you have done, and they have done, it illustrates how everything is in place, and yet they have not made it work. Unfortunately, you begin running around trying to get them to make less noise, and you end up losing time with your top performers, and then they start complaining, and the middle performers get the least amount of attention. You, the manager, have to be disciplined and you have to translate that into what you want out of them.

This reminded me of something that Thad Seligman of NAI said to me with great emphasis and profound impact: "Salespeople join organizations, but they leave managers." OB vehemently agrees.

JK: So, what, over time, has this three-tiered approach done for you and your managers?

OB: A few things.

1. It created the *right* turnover. People who leave are the ones who should leave. The right turnover helps the business grow, improves customer retention, and improves the value equation for customers. They will tell you about all the reps they had that were horrific. They will tell you the mistakes, the problems. By creating the right turnover, you have more of those magic moments, where everything works for the rep, the customer, and the company.

2. It makes the management process more efficient. You know who you are; you know where you are with the development of your team, and who is where. This tells you where your time needs to be spent, and you look at the business from a more efficient standpoint.

3. It helps managers understand how to be managers, because this makes sense to them.

Managers can be highly competitive, and if you can make a reference to their former life, whether as a salesperson or in their sports life, you can have them look around a room and identify who is an A, B, or C player and what they need to do to make an A player better, a B player better, and a C player figure out what they want to do.

C players are always in motion. They say they want to come to work for you; they ask for help; they seem to be trying to figure it out. You can point them to where they need to go, but you can't go there for them—they have to get there on their own two feet.

A sales manager is part sales leader, part coach, and part psychologist. The Three-Tiered Sales Team model is most powerful when writing business plans. I want people to label their team as A, B, or C players. When I push my managers into using these labels, it boils down to, "How are you going to get your people to change the level they are in or to maintain the level that they are in?"

I get them to think about the personality of the team and about how they will need to do things differently.

The larger percentage of head count exists in the center group. Top 10, bottom 10, and middle 80. It is rarely a third, a third, and a third.

Ultimate Sales Managers always understand where they need to go, which means, they understand:

♦ Where they are
♦ What is working
♦ What is *not* working
♦ What is a risk
♦ What is a threat
♦ Where there are opportunities
♦ How all of these relate to their customers, employees, and products

Ultimate Sales Managers go on sales calls with their salespeople. The goal of this experience is for the sales manager to create value for the salesperson. The sales manager should also understand where the opportunity lies to make the salesperson better. On each sales call, there is an opportunity to identify more prospects for the salesperson.

Ranking, performance reporting, or whatever your organization chooses to call it is an absolute *must* in OB's eyes. He says:

> We are a performance organization. That is how we are measured, monitored, and rewarded. Compensation plans are tied to performance, and bonus plans are tied to group performance, and there is incredible value in making sure that your peers understand the who, what, and where of performance. I have had more than one conversation over the years, where reps have come to me and said, "What are you doing? We all know this person is not working out."
>
> We want people who want to be successful, and the definition of success is meeting and exceeding the requirements the organization places on you when it comes to sales performance. You must give people a picture of where they are.
>
> By handing out leader boards every week, you can see who has new accounts, who has what dollar sales number, and so on. We are a performance organization.

Even though you have categorized your people according to this model, the "noisy" person OB refers to can live in any of the three tiers. It is a common refrain with OB, and with many of the other individuals interviewed here, that most sales managers have conversations with salespeople that revolve around what is preventing the individual salespeople from reaching their next level of performance rather than what they are doing correctly.

I asked him how that compares with the types of conversations he would prefer to have with his people. OB said:

> Sales managers must ask, "What do we need to fix, remove, or adapt for my sales team to be successful?"
>
> Reps say things like, "If you could _____, then I could sell more."

For example, "If I had better collateral, or better prices, or something along these lines, then I could sell more."

Salespeople will point out (or get "noisy" about) something that they want us to adapt, change, correct, or get rid of. They feel it is an impediment. My ideal conversation would sound more like this: "I was thinking. . . . I don't sell a lot of this, but I wonder if we could do . . ." This is a very useful conversation to me as a manager.

CROSS-POLLINATE YOUR TEAM

Categorizing does not mean that you should hold separate meetings, or have a different culture. The Ultimate Sales Manager wants good ideas, regardless of where they come from, to be shared with everyone in the group or on the team.

The culture in your group, team, or office is tangible and tenuous. It is something that visitors can identify immediately. The culture you work to create and maintain is an extension of your personality and view of what is acceptable, and what is not. If you listen to music at your desk, you are telling everyone, whether he or she has an open cube or a private office, that this is acceptable.

The three-tier model is about performance, not preferential treatment. It is about revenue planning and the right turnover. The culture should be reinforced with frank discussions, clear communication, and accountability. As your group is accountable to you, you are accountable to them to be their champion, their representative, and their confidant.

The three-tier model is one that should identify requirements for a salesperson's tenure and potential for advancement within your organization. OB used a reference to report cards earlier, and the three-tier model will impact the report card you receive from your superior, whether that person is a vice president, a C-level executive, or are the shareholders to whom you report.

Culture is the feel, the sound, the emotion, and the flavor of a sales team. Either people on the team buy into the culture or they don't. All of them contribute to it, simply by being an employee.

People influence each other, intentionally or otherwise. They have an impact on the health of your team, and you must be in touch with the impact, contribution, or detriment brought to the team by each person.

Attribute 16 of The Ultimate Sales Manager:
Learn some things about the sales job
that inspire people, and encourage your
folks to share them with the team.

You (and every member of your division) contribute to the culture and environment. In every instance, the sales manager has to establish the culture under which his sales office, department, or division is going to work.

To be an effective leader, you have to be aware of and in tune with your de facto leaders, putting them in a position to influence positively the team, or, you will have a situation like the one Thad Seligman recounted:

> I had a guy who made a million dollars a year, but no one in the office trusted or got along with him. I needed him because I needed his revenue, but he crossed the ethical line once (I won't say how), and it was too much for us. I had to release him. As a result, everyone in the office, over time, came to me and told me how thrilled he or she was that he was gone.
>
> We ended up not missing his revenue at all. *Everyone* stepped up, and we not only earned what he had earned, but more.
>
> The lesson for me was that even a top salesperson may be dragging you down, and you don't even realize it. It takes a long time to find that out. The big issue for us was that he was the antithesis of our culture, and I did not see it at first.
>
> It was fun to see what these folks could do, and I quickly recognized that there is no single individual, no matter how successful financially, who is so important that you turn your back on the basic culture of your team.

There is a larger company culture, but there will be a separate culture within the sales group. The culture of a successful sales team has to be one that fosters sharing, communication, working together, and helping one another be better at what they do. That may not necessarily be the culture of the rest of the company, but as the sales manager, you have to be the one to nurture your people.

Salespeople expect their sales manager to represent what it is that they go out and fight for every day. If you do not, and you represent just the money (and not the appropriate ethical behavior), the people you end up with are a bunch of unethical salespeople. The people who want an ethical environment will leave, and go and find it elsewhere.

The culture of the sales force is inherently based on the values and the culture of the sales manager and what that manager believes in as a professional.

By adapting and adopting the Three-Tiered Sales Team model and approach, you can divide your time more responsibly, be more responsive, focus your time and energy where it will be most useful, and ultimately achieve your goals.

Now that we have thought about getting the team to a manageable place, let's look at what we can do to offer incentives and accolades in Chapter 5.

5

REWARDS AND RECOGNITION

People go where they are wanted and stay where they are appreciated.
—Ed Friedman

Rewards and recognition are a fascinating aspect of the sales management function. The way you and I have to approach how we recognize our folks is different from any other profession. In medicine, someone is recognized for a profound discovery or for perfecting a life-saving procedure. In athletics, people are recognized for amazing feats of personal or team determination and excellence. Salespeople are recognized for doing their job.

When I first started in sales, I was not sure how it worked or what it required. In a reasonable amount of time, I closed my first deal. I was shocked, amazed, and thrilled. I was not sure exactly how it had happened, but I was being given credit for it, so I was really happy.

I went home and could not wait to tell my young bride about the spectacular feat that I had accomplished. I had closed a deal! I had made someone buy from me! When I told my wife, her response was, "That's your job."

The sense of deflation and disappointment over her not understanding or appreciating just how monumental my achievement was actually stopped me in my tracks.

She could see that I was underwhelmed with her reaction. (Salespeople are emotional, overanalytical, and so on.) Terri had worked as an emergency room trauma nurse for several years by the time we were married. She had seen her fair share of people on the brink of losing their life. She had been a participant in saving many, many lives. Closing a deal hardly compared to that, in her mind.

I mention this because in the minds of the salespeople you see walk into your office every day, closing a deal is a miraculous accomplishment. Closing several deals is cause for bands playing and parades marching by in their honor. Exceeding a quota is cause for television coverage.

I do not offer any of this tongue in cheek. I sell every day, and I have done so for many years. I understand what it takes. The strength to get up everyday and cold-call, the ability to recover from a deal looking like it will close and then falling apart at the eleventh hour, all of the possible disappointments and wrong turns that salespeople experience as part of their every day selling life are not foreign to me at any level.

So, we have to feed that unique aspect of someone's personality that has him show up daily, ready and willing to have the world try to pull the rug out from under him. We must find a way, gently and effectively, to applaud the efforts of someone who breaks into an account that has never been broken into before. We have to let these people know that what they do is worthy of note. This is done effectively in many ways.

Earlier, we pointed to a few key concepts, which inform the next few attributes of The Ultimate Sales Manager. One is confirmed throughout the book.

Attribute 17: Have recent, relevant selling experience.

This gives you credibility, and some insight into rewards and recognition. Next:

Attribute 18: Be 100 percent committed
to helping other people win.

As a leader and someone who sells constantly, The Ultimate Sales Manager combines or adopts these attributes, as well as Attribute 19.

Attribute 19: Understand that people will follow
someone they think is looking out for them.

When we recognize accomplishments, they cannot be only about the top performer, and the most amazing selling job done by the highest producers on the team. Salespeople need regular care and feeding, and I mean emotional feeding.

Telling someone that he sounded great on the phone today, or that the meeting you attended seemed to go well because of the way he handled it, will earn you motivational mileage. You can tap this emotional mileage, to help the person continue to improve, to develop as a professional, and to do the thing you want all of your folks to do—contribute to the team goal by exceeding their targets.

The great news is that when your folks exceed their targets, they earn more, they could reduce their stress, and your job becomes easier, because you now have one less person to worry about for this particular selling period.

I don't mean to put a damper on that upward swing of the previous paragraph, but you are only as good as your last reporting period, whether that is a week, a month, or a quarter. Measurement against goal, or quota, is your personal yardstick with your employer, like it or not. The Ultimate Sales Manager not only likes this aspect of the job, she embraces it.

In order to get a useful perspective of how you can use rewards and recognition to further your teams' accomplishments, I spoke to a few people with great track records as sales managers. Among many traits that are shared by each and every person interviewed for this book, one common and thrilling thread that runs through them all (and by extension, The Ultimate Sales Manager) is a passion for making the work that we do *fun*. Fun for us, fun for the people we are fortunate enough to work with, and fun for the people we, some day in the future, will manage.

When I asked Dennis Napoliello to participate, I knew that people who reported to him liked and performed for him.

So, we chose to discuss rewards and recognition. I started by asking Dennis: "What about the *fun?*"

RECOGNITION

Dennis said:

You have to make things fun. I tried and applied a lot of different ways of motivating people, both traditional and nontraditional.

We created and conducted contests. Not only on a monthly basis, but quarterly. We also tracked for president's circle, and recognized the status of people at a monthly kick off. Depending on what we were trying to accomplish, we might center our goals around a weekly contest, a "get-out-of-the-gate" contest, trying to motivate people to keep their eye on the ball. With a 10-person sales team, I would do 5 on 5 matches. Now, understand that this was all in fun, and the people who participated enjoyed it. We were not offending anyone.

We had a "meat-and-beans" contest—the idea was to pit individual performers against each other. Salespeople *love* competition because they not only want to win, they *expect* to win. We would have a celebration or recognition dinner, and the people who won would eat steak, and the others would eat beans. We had some fun there—people know it is in fun.

We also did some nontraditional stuff like "monthly heroes." We had a *Terminator* action figure that we used as a memento to the sales rep who gets hit from every different angle, maybe gets a lot of challenges, and who comes out of it in good shape. He was "the Terminator," meaning that he won the award, and was required to bring the doll to every meeting until someone else won it.

From a motivation standpoint, a lot of people center rewards and recognition around money and contests, but you get just as much out of the steps you take to recognize the little things people do as any amount of cash or prizes.

For instance, when you know that someone has been trying to win an appointment with a certain account, and he finally does, you walk by his desk, unexpectedly, and congratulate him on that specific achievement. That moment can go as far with motivating your staff as a $1,000 bonus.

Sometimes, the best way to motivate is to make sure that people have visual representations of what they want to win. We had a contest where there would be a $1,000 bonus, and it seemed tired after a while, but I sent the sales managers reporting to me out to speak to all of their salespeople to find out what they would do with the money, if they won it. We had them print out or draw in their own hand what they were going to buy if they won the $1,000 bonus.

What motivates people is so different, and it was a great way to keep people focused. The person who won the award one quarter was someone who wanted a snow blower. Now, everyone is different, and if it were up to me, I would not be that excited about a snow blower, but *he was*, and that is all that counts. It showed me that when you understand what is really important to your folks, you really can go that much further, because it is about them. Visualization is important.

It is difficult to get sales managers to go out on appointments with their reps, for some reason. As a sales director, with several managers reporting to me in the past, I found that frustrating. So, I thought, well, I am going to go out, roll up my sleeves, and go knock on some doors with some of the reps. I think it is important for the leadership to do the exact job that we are asking the salespeople to do.

Constant involvement is important, but more important, as a sales manager, you should never ask your salespeople to do something that you would not be willing or able to do yourself.

Continuing the trend of sales managers I spoke to, Dennis felt it was "essential" that a sales manager have personal selling experience. It affords credibility, and when you have personally sold for a living, you do more than empathize when someone has lost a potential sale, or a customer has stopped buying from her due to corporate changes or a million other things that salespeople experience daily.

Jennifer Yester is one of the smartest, most dynamic, and unsinkable people I have ever had the pleasure to know. She recruited me into my first position as a sales manager. Jennifer is the president and CEO of A+, The Employment Company, a staffing and employment firm specializing in the entertainment industry.

She and I spoke about being sales managers, and I asked her the question I asked many other people in preparation for this book: "Who in their right mind would want to go to work every day and manage salespeople?"

After a trademarked hearty laugh, Jennifer said:

My therapist and I are working through that right now!

Actually, the thing that keeps me wanting to come back every day is that it is rewarding, fun, and exciting. It is not a tangible thing that you do—it can be disappointing, but it can also be very rewarding to help someone grow, develop, and achieve things. To get someone to buy into your goals and objectives is very rewarding. Salespeople are driven by feelings and managers by the bottom line. I do feel that there is an emotional reward in managing salespeople.

If I am servicing my customers and I am filling their needs, getting them the people who they need to perform a function, and doing it well, that is something that I love doing. It's simple: Taking care of my clients' needs turns into dollar signs. I am more driven by the bottom line than I am driven by feeling good.

Rewards and recognition are not about getting people to do something unique or special—it is about what is going to work for them. If my biggest thing is that I want everyone to know that I am the number-one seller, money in my paycheck may not work for me as well as the announcements and the recognition.

I have to know who the salesperson is, what gets him excited, and find a way to recognize and to reward what is meaningful and powerful to that person. For one person, it might be an afternoon off to spend with his children, but for another it might be the opportunity to leave early on Friday to go to a dog show. I cannot manage the whole team as one entity.

The Ultimate Sales Manager should reward people on an individual basis. Recognition is a personal issue. Since salespeople are generally driven by their feelings, and we, as sales managers, are generally driven by the bottom line, numbers, and producing, these two have to mesh together.

The single most important thing that I have found that impacts people is to reward them in front of their peers. Offering a special dinner or giving them a plaque puts them in a position where they have an audience, and salespeople love having an audience.

JK: How do you keep track of what to do and offer regarding each of your people?

JY: I keep profiles on each of my people, which are not unlike what my hairdresser does with me. Each time I go, she has a card that she pulls out when I come in, and she knows what color and style, what she did for me last time I was there, and what I like.

I keep a profile on file like the information I maintain regarding my clients. What are their dog's names? What are their kids' names and ages? What is important to them? What are their goals?

I have a salesperson who has a goal to buy a house within the next calendar year, so she is really motivated by money. I have another person with the goal of being able to work three days a week and maintain her income. I love these files.

JK: What have you done that has gotten you the biggest bang for your buck?

JY: Walking out in front of the team, when everyone is in the office, and making an announcement about details of what someone has done. It is more powerful and *works better than money*—it is better than more time off. That one little gesture of making her feel like she is just outstanding in front of her peers, her coworkers, is far more than anything else I could do. More than Christmas gifts, bonuses—anything.

It is my job as the manager to know how this month compares to last, or this quarter compares to last. Salespeople don't really care. That commission is already spent, and that is ancient history. We have a lot more currency than commissions, bonuses, and so on.

Tying incentives and rewards to performance will only work if you are very clear with your staff about what it will take to earn a reward or incentive. You have to know where your people stand in a contest or challenge—you should be able to answer them on your feet.

We keep a chalkboard with everyone's name. It indicates where people are, how they are progressing, and it is where everyone can see it. Everyone on my sales team looks at that every morning, and I see it as a motivating tool.

JK: So, the environment in your office is the result of a specific idea or plan on your part?

JY: Absolutely. Three words to describe my sales environment and our sales culture have always been:

1. Happy
2. Fun
3. Successful

If folks are happy, and they are having fun, it means that we are successful and the company is making money.

Rewards and recognition can come out of your annual budget, or they come out of your creative mind and your supportive, encouraging mouth.

Very few people I have spoken with regarding this topic felt that there was one *best* way to do this, but there were common threads, as described here in this chapter. We use rewards and recognition to add to the fun quotient. We use them because we know that people feed on them.

We set up in our mind what the expectations of all of our folks are, and we stay close to them, offering encouragement, answers, and solutions. However, there are some people, no matter what The Ultimate Sales Manager does, tries, thinks, or uses who will simply not get the job done. They will be so close ("I have a deal coming any moment," they cry), and yet they do not seem to get over the finish line. Or they are a bad influence, regardless of their numbers and achievement.

The bottom line is that they need to go, and you need to fire them. So, let's move to Chapter 6 and determine when to fire a salesperson.

WHEN TO FIRE A SALESPERSON

As a manager, more specifically as a sales manager, you have an impossible job. You have immeasurable variables pointing toward your next achievement. While quotas and goals may occupy most of your thinking, knowing when, how, and why someone should be removed from the team will be part of your job, as well. Even though we cannot keep someone on board because we are nervous that he or she will go to a competitor, that possibility exists at all times, with all levels of performers.

Attribute 20: Make decisions as if your closest competitor is sitting on your shoulder.

To me, that means that how you treat your people, who you keep, and who you release will be known to your competitors. Your management style is probably being described to someone as you read this. Your closest competitor may be able to become an ally at some level, by helping you understand motivation and decision making among the salespeople circulating in your industry or market.

The Ultimate Sales Manager must know when it is time to fire someone. You, in pursuit of becoming The Ultimate Sales Manager must be decisive, and once you know in your heart and head that someone must leave the organization, you need to take the steps to make it happen as soon as possible. Every day that you have someone on board that everyone (including you) knows should leave, is a day spent rationalizing and making excuses.

Attribute 21: Never delay or procrastinate when bad news must be delivered.

There is nothing pleasant about firing someone, and although people offer various anecdotes and euphemisms to make it less unpleasant, it is distasteful, uncomfortable, and simply just not fun. In addition, I have never found anyone with character who enjoyed firing people. This is not a decision that should be taken lightly, nor should it be made as the result of an emotional whim.

You may do everything you can to create an upbeat, fun, and professional environment, but the harsh reality is that some folks are just not going to work out. This means that they must be fired, and you will have to do it.

You may have an HR representative there to cover paperwork and make sure that you dot all of the Is, but you will have to do some or most of the talking. This means looking an employee in the eye and telling her that her desk has already been cleaned out and that she is no longer employed.

In this scenario, it may seem that you are putting her in the position of having to face the following week unemployed. But wait, are *you* putting her in that position? I don't think so. People know what the sales profession is about—it is about performance. If there are no deals on the board, there is no revenue coming in with that person's name on it.

It is not as graphic or attention getting as "survival of the fittest" displays in documentaries about predators and their prey, but let's not sugarcoat it. Salespeople are employed to sell, and anything short of that is unacceptable. Chefs do not stand in the kitchen, talking about preparing a meal; they deliver. My gardener is not paid because he is trying to figure out the best way to approach the tasks I have asked him to do. He gets those tasks done.

Some of the people I spoke to in preparation for this book recounted various stories about people who almost seemed relieved when they were told that they were being "let go." While I have never personally experienced that type of reaction, I have been called names and have been accused of various personality or judgment flaws. But these all were the result of someone's immediate and angered reaction to this news.

Almost everyone I know and everyone I have ever spoken to about firing salespeople has come to the same conclusion: If a salesperson is being let go, it should not be a shock to him. If you have done your job as their manager, you have walked him through actions and consequences, deadlines, expectations, and all of the things that are required of him. If this news comes as a shock and the individual thinks that everything is fine, regardless of the fact that he has not met a single objective laid out for him, there is a deficiency in perception that you as a manager cannot ever (nor should you spend *any* of your valuable time trying to) fix.

Frank Phillips of RN Network had some interesting comments about firing salespeople:

> One of the most difficult things is to know for sure when to cut the cord and when to hang on a little longer. There may be many variables, but not so many that you cannot make an informed decision. It may be informed, but it is still hard.
>
> I look beyond just the numbers before I let someone go; you have to look at what someone is going through during the time that person is struggling. Are there distractions at home? Is he having a hard time with something? We have to get an idea of this before we just cut him loose. The reason being is that it is much

easier to rectify a salvageable employee than to start all over again with someone new. If he is "keepable," it is easier to work with him and hold onto him, than it is to go out, hire someone new, teach him the job, teach him the culture, and expect results. It takes a while to see results in our environment.

However, if someone just does not get it, and he or she walks in and out of the office at the same time everyday like clockwork, yet nothing changes, and nothing improves—it is this simple: If his heart is not in this work, I cannot want it for him.

It has parallels to parenting, because the employee has control. I tell people regularly: If you do not get up every Monday and look forward to coming in here, this may not be for you. You have to have a passion for this. If someone does not have passion for this work, he or she is not going to be successful. We have to believe that the nurses we put in these hospitals are having a good positive impact.

We are selling relationships here. We want to place that nurse over and over again. We do not want to work with a hospital once—we want to work with it many times. In that regard, it is truly a relationship.

As The Ultimate Sales Manager, you will have gone a long and sometimes difficult path with people, before ultimately (no pun intended) deciding to release them. There are millions of euphemisms for this process, from "letting them go" to "allowing them to pursue a career elsewhere."

As important as it is to have a sense of humor about the work that you do, when you walk into the meeting that will end someone's tenure with you and your organization, it must be done with a straight face, the most professional approach, and the other person's dignity and personal feelings in full view. Follow Attribute 22 of The Ultimate Sales Manager.

Attribute 22: Be aware of the delivery, receipt, and perception of your message—*always*.

Let's review what should be done—the steps that lead you to the point where you ask the salesperson into a conference room with the HR representative. In many organizations today, it is essential that a representative from HR attend this conversation. You need someone to keep the conversation unemotional, professional, and most important, brief and to the point.

So, prior to this meeting, let's count backward to where the end of a salesperson's career with you and your organization began. We have already addressed, and you have implemented, the following steps of the employment cycle:

♦ From the beginning of the interview process, before this person was even offered a job, you ensured that she knew the position for which you were hiring her. You specifically defined the duties, expectations, measurement for performance criteria, and chain of command.

♦ You interviewed according to a system that would allow more than one person in your organization to meet this person and give you an evaluation as to how she would fit into the current culture.

♦ You invested time, some more time, and an extra helping of even more time in training and developing this person.[1]

♦ You have walked this person through a specific performance evaluation, and you made sure that your expectations were clear.

♦ If this person accomplished something of note, you recognized her for it.

♦ If this person strayed off the path, you brought her back.

♦ You made as objective an evaluation as you could about where she landed in the three-tier matrix (see Chapter 4).

♦ All of the facts, details, gut senses, and hallway conversations with this person have made it abundantly clear to you that she needs to go.

---

[1] This doesn't mean that they have to have been on board for months upon months. Many managers tell me that they know in the first 30 days if someone will make it. By "training," I mean you have not sent them out into the jungle to "figure it out on their own."

You can look at this checklist and think, "That is a lot to go through, just to make sure that the person needs to leave." And I sit here in vehement agreement with you, because your people are your job.

Jennifer Yester told me years ago:

> As managers, our inventory walks out the door every night. You are charged with the care, development, discipline, learning, success, health, and well-being of some amazing people. Many of them may amaze you in how they can appear to be working, yet there are not any tangible results.
>
> I have seen companies keep people on their payroll for *over a year* without any profit generated from that person's effort. This is beyond baffling to me. It is akin to parents of an unruly child acting as if they have no idea how the child learned such behavior. If your people are not producing, it is *someone's* fault. Guess who you need to examine first?

◆

I realize as I write this that this is one of the shortest chapters in the book, and that should tell us something. The shortest distance between two points is a straight line. Once your gut tells you that someone has to go, your next steps should be clear.

As we mentioned in Chapter 4, the people in your bottom tier should always be "in motion"—either moving up toward the middle tier, or on their way out of your organization. With these people, you apply regular pressure. You ask them more questions, more often. You lengthen your one-on-one meetings. You show genuine concern, while doing everything you can to make sure that they know they are underperforming.

You do not point it out to them each day, but you do ask what he thinks will happen, you ask how the selling day looks from his perspective. This kind of pressure is fitting and necessary. As you apply further pressure, you will know quickly if he has chosen to respond to this pressure by moving up, moving out, or hoping that you will make a dramatic decision for him.

While I advocate applying pressure to salespeople, I do not recommend applying it to all of them, and not as an overall management style, and not all of the time. However, some individuals thrive under pressure. Often, the top performers tend to create their own pressure, putting themselves under pressure to perform, maintain a top ranking, or beat the rookies.

Consistently producing salespeople are the hardest to find and the best to have. They elevate what the other team members aspire to, responding to your pressure by performing.

KNOW THY TEAM

Hiring people, managing them, coaching them, and losing them adds up to a lot of work. Remember Attribute 23 of The Ultimate Sales Manager.

Attribute 23: Do not expect people who work *for* you to work *like* you.

The delicate balance of understanding your sales team, being sensitive to who they are, how they operate, what motivates them, and other factors is the key to your success with and retention of good people. Maintaining this balance means knowing when you can exert pressure, and on whom to apply it, to get the results you need.

When pressure does not motivate the people you are concerned about, it will become apparent that since they are not moving up to the bread-and-butter, or B, group in your three-tiered system (even with your added time and attention), they must be moved out.

Many managers have told me that it is almost a relief when someone comes to them and announces that they have found something else, are going to the competition, or have decided to go back to the family farm (it could happen!). It is rarely a surprise when salespeople are "let go."

During this stage in the employment cycle, you may encounter people who are convinced that all they need is that one deal or order to take them over the hump. They use phrases like, "I know something is going to pop soon," "I can feel a deal, it's just a matter of time," or other hopeful, yet painfully vague avoidance techniques. As a sales manager, you have to maintain a delicate balance between dreams and reality, between fantasy and a specific number of recorded phone calls.

Todd Katler, director of sales with Rent.com, leads a group of 20 salespeople who are geographically spread across the United States. These individuals use an online contact management software called Salesforce.com. This tool is amazing, because it gives everyone in Todd's group good intelligence, access to leads, and most important, it tracks all of the activity they generate. Amazingly, it only tracks the activity that the salespeople enter into the system under their disciplined approach and Todd's urging. He has a simple retort for discussions with people whose activity is low: *"If it isn't in Salesforce, it doesn't exist."*

This is one of those statements that salespeople may attempt to argue with, but the simple fact is that Todd goes out of his way to communicate the importance (actually, to use his word "necessity") of tracking the activity each salesperson generates. Since they are spread across the country, he can hardly watch them work. He is in no position to observe their amazingly disciplined work habits, nor can he see how long they have worked on a proposal.

All he can see is what they record, how much time they invest, and what the results are at the end of the month. Todd says that after three months of substandard performance, you have to assume that it is *not* the tools, the product, the pricing, or the economy. It is the salesperson that is not working out.

This is not an enjoyable part of the job. It never will be. The first time I fired someone, I was sick about it for days. I found myself wondering how he was going to pay his bills, what his family was going to do, and a variety of other guilt-ridden thoughts about the process. The first salesperson I fired made it very easy on me. He quietly looked me in the eye, called me a "jerk," took his final check, and walked out. I say he made it easy on me because I was fully aware of what lead to his being fired: He had not done his job.

That evening, as every evening, I discussed the experience in detail with my wife. "How can he blame me for his own performance?" I howled. "He did not do what was expected of him, and it's *my* fault?" You and I both know that anything that happens in your department, under your watch (whether you are in the room when it happens or not), is your fault. I am not playing the tortured executive here—I am taking on the role of the responsible party.

When I led small teams of men in the navy, whatever they did was my responsibility. When I ran battlefield communications in the Sea Bees, I had a few people reporting to me. It was my job to check out their radios every day, to go over the codes of conduct for the day, reexamine the battle plan, and ensure that no one would say anything over the radio that was unprofessional, or worse, could alert the enemy to any details about our location, the size of the battalion, or anything else that should not go out over the airwaves.

Being a group of young, playful, peacetime, military men, a couple of them decided to push the envelope. They started to goof around and see what they could get away with. It sounds childish, I know, but we were living in dirt on a military installation in Northern California for nine days, and it was uncomfortable to say the least. They were looking for any entertainment they could find.

I was in my early 20s, and I had to find these men, relieve them of duty, and speak about their behavior to the commanding officer in front of our whole squad. These were men whom I had gone drinking with in Spain, just a few months before, men who had made fun of my New York accent, and I was the one who laughed the hardest. But when it was time to go to work, and time for me to take on the responsibility of leading my team, I had no choice but to make it very clear that I was going to follow orders, and I expected everyone in my group to do the same.

Leadership may not be fun, and it was an ugly few hours after these men received disciplinary action, but eventually, a few of them treated me with more respect. I may not have been their closest friend after that, but the ones who understood why I held my ground and who started taking their job more seriously were the ones I ended up having the best relationships with throughout the remainder of my naval career.

ULTIMATE CONSISTENCY

The actions, attitudes, reactions, and mental approach to the job your sales team is assigned are a direct reflection of the environment you establish and maintain daily. If your emotions waver, or are erratic, and it is difficult for them to know what sort of mood you will be in, or how you will react to news they bring you (good or bad), it will be difficult for them to be comfortable bringing you *any* news. The delicate balance you must maintain here involves working for some harmony in their working environment, which by default is dictated by yours.

When it is time to fire someone, most often, both of you will know it. Some people have difficulty admitting to themselves, their employers, or their families that a particular company or career may not be for them. If you hire someone based strictly on her fun and dynamic personality, keep in mind that she may have been performing for you, thinking that those attributes are what make a good salesperson.

The outside influences that lead someone to apply for a sales job are innumerable. Hence, the interview question: "What does your family think of you pursuing a career in sales?" I know that it took some time for my wife to adjust to the trials and tribulations, the peaks and valleys, of the salesperson's life.

CHANGE IS PART OF THE JOB

You are going to lose people. This does not mean you are not a competent manager. Salespeople in a free economy have every right to see if they can get a better deal elsewhere. So, when they do, they know they will be leaving.

Remember that Thad Seligman of NAI keeps a specific mantra in mind at all times:

People join companies, but they leave managers.

In some cases, salespeople are going to quit, in others, they are going to be fired. In still others, they are going to fire you as their manager, but you *cannot* allow them to stay after they have. Salespeople who are managed by The Ultimate Sales Manager know what they are expected to do and achieve and how they are to comport themselves. Should they fall short, the consequences are not mysterious or a surprise.

You must remove the cancer that is known as the unresponsive salesperson. If you are a fanatic about attendance at meetings, reporting, or participation, but you have a high-producing salesperson who just cannot seem to find the office in time for the beginning of the meeting, you are sending a specific message to every other person on your team that performance trumps participation.

If this is part of your plan, and you can look someone in the eye and say that this is how you want people to operate, then that's fine. But if it is not, you are at fault for allowing it to continue. You must either corral and get participation from that person or determine how to replace the revenue that he or she brings to the table.

Thad Seligman goes on to say:

> I would rather have an empty seat than an empty suit. The person who comes in every day and does not work is telling everyone else that this type of behavior is acceptable.
>
> If you have people who are not cutting it, and you do not release them, you are doing them (and your team, and your company, and the customers that person interacts with) a disservice.
>
> Many people have made careers of mediocrity in sales, but they may have had more personal satisfaction in something else. It hurts sometimes to fire people. I have never let anyone go who did

not come back and say thank you. I have also had good, ongoing relationships with people that I have let go.

There are a few principles that you can keep in mind when preparing for this most unpleasant aspect of your job—firing a salesperson:

◆ *Maintain the person's dignity.*
◆ *Do not get involved in an argument or debate.*
◆ *Keep your voice even.*
◆ *Let the person vent.* He or she will calm down eventually. Maybe not in your office, or in the conference room where you have this conversation, or even before leaving the building, but he or she will calm down.
◆ *Have all of your documentation in order.* Make sure that nothing you say can be contested or can be shown to be short of actual fact.
◆ *Once you decide, act.* Do not put it off.
◆ *Have a sense of timing.* The holidays are hardly the best time of year to let someone go.
◆ *Stay focused on the discussion.* No cell phones, no ringing conference phone in the room, and make sure that no one interrupts you. Have your assistant or someone guard the door to the room to deflect any potential inadvertent intrusions.
◆ *Do not tell yourself that you are helping the person by keeping him or her on staff.* Each day that goes by where someone is in the wrong job is a disservice. Once you decide that someone has to go, fire him or her.
◆ *Do not allow the person to go back to his or her desk immediately after your discussion.* Have any personal effects packed by someone else, in plain view of everyone who works near this person.
◆ *Do not act like it did not happen at the next sales meeting.*

♦ *Do not respond emotionally to anything the person being fired says, even if it is a personal attack.* Yes, people do say things that you might not expect or like to hear.

♦ *Do not do anything that will give the person ammunition to paint you as unprofessional.* All of your conduct, with the people in your department, or who report to you, is on full display at all times. Conversations you have with Phil will get back to Mary. Count on it. Do not compromise your authority as a leader with questionable activities.

When you fire people (and you will), your team will look to you for direction, commitment, and vision. They look for reassurance that the team, the day, and their individual lives will go on. Many will look very closely at their recent performance. (Firing someone is an attention getter. People see someone walking out the door, and potentially wonder if they are candidates for release.)

There is a lot of good that you will see and experience after someone who is not performing leaves. The team might become closer. They may go out of their way for each other more often. My favorite was the short time where there was more work going on than discussion of work. There were more calls being made than stories being told about calls. In short, the environment would actually brighten.

MOVING FORWARD

It is unrealistic to assume that your team will stay the same throughout your tenure, regardless of its length. You can be assured that whatever the head count, whoever your top performers may be, whichever people concern you, or whatever the marketplace's pending changes may be, you will have to gather together with your folks regularly.

Sales meetings are the sole topic of Part II. We address two types of sales meetings:

1. *Group meetings.* The ones you regularly lead with the entire team.
2. *One-on-one meetings.* The time when you sit one on one with each person on the team and get a chance to really find out where he is, where he has been, and where he thinks he is going.

PART II

Sales Meetings

7

GROUP MEETINGS

Ahh . . . the weekly sales meeting. What joy, what fun, what a *drag*! There are few challenges in the litany of duties of The Ultimate Sales Manager as taxing, trying, and frustrating as preparing for, the running of, and receiving feedback about the weekly sales meeting.

Sales meetings are part of the job, and The Ultimate Sales Manager makes meetings work for her, her staff, and the company's objectives. Sales meetings are exercises in discipline, focus, listening, teaching, and team building. Many salespeople dread sales meetings, because, unfortunately, they are usually run poorly. This is not the sales manager's time to pontificate. Rather, it is time to communicate, teach, and inspire. All of the more esoteric aspects of what you do come to the fore in these assemblies.

Since the team meeting is the main forum in which you actively lead and train your team, it is here that you must display the characteristics you strive for as The Ultimate Sales Manager. In Chapter 8, we discuss the one-on-one meetings you will conduct with your team and the elements that are important in that environment.

Your goals during team meetings are to:

- ◆ Inspire
- ◆ Instruct
- ◆ Educate
- ◆ Inform
- ◆ Entertain
- ◆ Challenge
- ◆ Recognize
- ◆ Visualize

TEAM VISUALIZATION

This list of goals should remind you that your meetings are your opportunity to create an enthusiasm for your vision among your people. You will not realize a vision without your salespeople's belief in the vision, you, and themselves. It is much more fun to achieve your vision with and through them, than working yourself to death with no reward.

The Ultimate Sales Manager makes it a priority to increase sales, while balancing people's lives. Sales meetings are your forum to communicate your vision to your team. They are part performance, part instruction. They are part open forum, part rumor central. They are ultimately (love that word) where you are under the most scrutiny and therefore must regularly shine.

STRUCTURING AND PLANNING

Team meetings are where you offer ideas and inspiration for your sales people to go out and fight the good fight. This is where you casually mention which ranking someone has and how that matches up with regional or national rankings of performance throughout your company. Team sales meetings are demanding and intimidating, but they also give you a forum in which you can hone your skills at conducting and leading them because you have to do it regularly.

Scott Knorp, one of the most successful sellers of headsets, video conferencing, and ancillary products in the country, is also

President of a company called Quagga. His company provides these products and services to Fortune 1,000 companies across the United States. Scott and I met over 10 years ago when he was the vice president of sales for another company that operates in this selling space, and while he held the vice president title, he also sold more than anyone else in that company.

Scott is a relationship seller, with a great, self-effacing sense of humor. He is a big proponent of the concept, "Take what you do as a manager seriously, but do not take yourself seriously."

He and I spoke about his approach to sales meetings. Scott is still selling, and he walks a fine line as a player/coach. That fine line means that he is still close enough to the selling function (i.e., it affects his income) to have similar concerns to the people who report to him. We spoke about a variety of issues, and Scott, as a player/coach, has to be consistent, and he is a living example of Attribute 22: Be aware of the delivery, receipt, and perception of your message—*always*, as well as Attribute 23: Do not expect some people who work *for* you to work *like* you. Let's hear what he has to say:

> I want people to get specific things out of sales meetings, like new techniques, or what someone else who is selling the same product might be doing. Salespeople avoid sales meetings due to having to publicly air where they fell short. I am very sensitive to the fact that salespeople do not want their time wasted, so it must be useful info.

People make mistakes when planning or conducting a sales meeting, including:

♦ Making it too much about them (the manager)
♦ Focusing on issues that are too removed from the actual selling activities

Scott is committed to focus and fun in his meetings. He describes them as free-for-alls in which anyone can contribute. He also asks that during a sales quarter, every salesperson invite a guest speaker.

SK: This gets people thinking in advance about the meetings, and we have had some great people join us. They get to know us a bit more, and we walk away with some information we might not have gotten elsewhere.

JK: So, tell me about the fun.

SK: You mean the gong?

JK: Yes.

SK: We have a small gong that is to be rung as soon as anyone (me, my partners, a salesperson, or guest speaker) has gone over their allotted time. The fun thing is that it keeps everyone on their toes, and paying attention. It's almost like a contest, to see who will ring the gong. It keeps us focused, and its fun.

KEEPING PEOPLE INTERESTED

Bob Dean is someone who demonstrates Attribute 24 of The Ultimate Sales Manager.

**Attribute 24: Be the first to offer help or a joke,
and the last to give up.**

As such, he has a unique perspective on sales meetings. This is not surprising, considering that he has been conducting them for 30 years:

The problem with sales meetings is that salespeople are action people. They want to get from point A to point B. There is a reason they are good at what they do—it is because they tend to be easily distracted. They will follow any shiny object.

This is, however, part of the reason that we love them. They are action oriented; they will run down the street at a moment's urging, without even knowing why they are going—it just seemed like a good idea.

Salespeople, when new to a team (regardless of age) tend to be eager and full of enthusiasm. They jump into activities or conversations at inappropriate times, in the hope of becoming part of the group as soon as possible. I have had experiences like those that Bob describes with different salespeople, which also remind me of some experiences from the navy. I remember serving with HS-6, a helicopter squadron, on board the *USS Constellation* in 1980.

Whenever you were new to anything in the navy, you were referred to as a "boot camp," or simply "boot." This was not meant as a term of endearment. In the navy, as in all of the most successful organizations, experience is held in high esteem, particularly in the harsher, more stressful environments, such as when an aircraft carrier is at sea.

I remember an incident that occurred after I had been on board for a few months. I was in the Ready Room (this is where flight plans, orders of the day, and all meetings were conducted having to do with the leadership and operation of our squadron) one day, and a new arrival (a "boot") came in. This room was fascinating to me, because I could listen in on nonclassified briefings, and learn about the squadron's function and responsibility. I was not the only one who liked to hang out there, and the new arrival was excited and curious. A Chief Petty Officer (a significantly ranked enlisted man) came in after him and the Chief knew, just by looking at the kid, that he didn't know where he was or if he belonged there. Navy Chief Petty Officers are experienced, knowledgeable, and full of vinegar. They love to play with the new people on board.

This Chief thought it would be entertaining to send the Boot on an impossible errand—

"Hey Boot!" he barked.

"Sir?" the kid replied.

"Go get me the keys to the helicopter! The CO is waiting on deck!"

This kid took off so fast that he banged his head and knee running through the hatch. He was so excited that he was three compartments away before he slowed down, and two decks closer to the flight deck before it hit him: He had no idea what the keys to the helicopter looked like or (more important) where they could be found.

The Chief was laughing so hard he couldn't drink his coffee for about five minutes. After a while, I had heard him tell the story enough, so I left the ready room. I saw the kid asking people where he might find these elusive keys, and thought—he will *never* live this down. Why? Because there *are no* keys to helicopters! The poor kid just wanted to be a part of what was going on, and in his enthusiasm, he did not bother to get the specifics that would have been necessary for the task.

◆

Salespeople can be like this, but thankfully most sales managers do not have the light-hearted mean streak that the Chief had. Bob Dean likes to make sure that his people are not running out to get the keys to the helicopter, and he wants them to look forward to sales meetings. Meetings are part of how he manages, and they are instrumental in how he establishes the environment his office enjoys.

Bob Dean's Five Golden Rules for Sales Meetings

1. *Set a common goal.* Constantly measure performance against the sales objectives of the team.
2. *Limit length to one hour.*
3. *Teach or tell them three things that they don't know.* Try to tie the new information (i.e., changes in procedures or pricing) into something that you are sure that they do not know.
4. *Make them laugh three times.*
5. *Memorize some of the numbers you will deliver.* Even if you have bullets on the screen, take it to the next level—memorize numbers that may not be on the screen. If you use that as a tool to recognize someone, to point out who is the national leader, and to place your local folks in comparison to national ranking, without looking at a piece of paper, it makes them feel appreciated. It takes less than a minute to memorize, but it will have 24 hours of value as a leader. It illustrates how im-

portant that information is. It carries a much stronger connotation for the folks you recognize.

Some clarification: Bob has many sources for the "make them laugh three times" part of how he prepares for his sales meetings, and they are available to all of us. He and I (and many other people I have spoken to) have used the Internet to find funny, clean, relevant cartoons or jokes that you can share during meetings. Many of your colleagues or friends will also be willing to keep you in the loop if they find something funny that you can use. Your friends or other sales managers in your company or industry may have similar items, and when you are on the lookout for such things, you encounter them much more often.

WHAT'S THE PRIORITY?

Every meeting should begin and end by touching on the same topic (tell them what you are going to tell them; tell them; then tell them what you told them). This creates a closed loop on the information shared, and it ensures that people know your priorities. Bob Dean says that making everything a priority makes nothing a priority:

> You can't stand up and say: "Listen up, this is really important," and then make that the preface to the next statement, too. You reduce how important each statement is. When you roll something off that is powerful information, you automatically make it important in their minds.

PREPARATION + PROFESSIONALISM = PRODUCTIVITY

I will say it again, because it is that important: Prepare in advance for your meetings. Your preparation is obvious, and your lack of preparation can be downright *painful*. Preparation demonstrates that a sales manager has vision. Salespeople will think, "This person not only prepares for the meeting but also stands without paper and quotes rankings off the top of his head." It shows vision because the sales manager is familiar enough with and versed enough in this information to have it at his fingertips. It shows vision because it is clear that the sales manager is aware of where his team is, where they need to be, and what they need to achieve to get there.

IF IT WERE EASY, EVERYONE WOULD DO IT

I have often referred to sales meetings that I have led as "wrestling matches" because it is mentally and physically taxing to keep people interested, especially if they feel their time could be better spent elsewhere. Salespeople want to be in control of their time and activities, and when you involve them in policy or procedure discussions, they will either battle you at every opportunity or drag things out for their own enjoyment.

Bob Dean sees sales meetings as the time to reinforce the sense of environment and comportment that he works for every time he walks through the office or interacts with his team. He is very careful not to allow things to go off topic:

> Whenever someone says in a meeting or a discussion that "the company is _____" I stop them and ask them to rephrase. I say, "Don't say 'the company' because that refuses to put a face on it. If you have a complaint or an issue, don't say, 'the company' say, 'Bob Dean'." It helps them to express what the problem is, and it helps me to make sure that they see me as "the company." I do not remove or distance myself from corporate mandates.
>
> Whether I agree with everything that the company does is not the issue—the issue is that, as a manager for my company, I have to demonstrate loyalty, and I have to take ownership of the company mandates and directives. That is the only way I can lead and set expectations.

To me, power is the desire and willingness to take on responsibility. Thus, Attribute 25 of The Ultimate Sales Manager.

> **Attribute 25: Never side with your folks against "the company." *You* are the company—so talk about news, changes, and updates as if you fully support them, because you *must*.**

TIMING IS EVERYTHING

Other managers and people interviewed for this book have opinions about meetings as well. Jennifer Yester has led meetings of all sizes, under a variety of conditions. She and I worked together for a company during a time when the corporate owner decided to refurbish the office with us in it. The environment was loud, distracting, and dusty, yet we found a way to focus and keep selling.

She has led meetings with one or two people, when she went into business for herself, and she has led meetings with a diverse group of business owners and leaders as part of her tenure as president of the California Association of Staffing.

She told me, "Sales meetings need to be focused on motivating and teaching, period. When we start to talk about individual problems, like one or two people not producing, that is the wrong place for those discussions."

Timing is important. Begin and *end* on time. Jennifer also says, "Weekly sales meeting should be 30 minutes tops. You want to motivate them, teach them, recognize them, and that is motivating. When we go to conferences, and we hear something useful or motivational, meetings are a great time to share these ideas with the team. Rewards and recognition should be marched out whenever it is appropriate. Sales meetings require you to be prepared and professional if you want them to be productive."

Jennifer, Bob, Scott, and I all believe in the necessity and power of regular sales meetings. Getting the group together consistently creates the dynamic of opening dialogue that might not occur on the selling floor. Take the time in sales meetings to quell rumors. Take the time to hear one or two folks out. Take the time to ask someone in advance to participate as a speaker or instructor. Ultimately, take the time to prepare.

You may not find the time or opportunity to share everything you want to share during a specific meeting, and that is okay. Make sure that you keep it on your list for the next meeting. I have seen many sales managers with large files of "meeting ideas." This is wise, considering that they keep coming up.

In Chapter 8, we show you a format for the meetings in between the group sales meetings—the one on one. I call these Fifteen Minutes of Fame™.

8

ONE-ON-ONE MEETINGS—FIFTEEN MINUTES OF FAME

In the future, everyone will be famous for 15 minutes.

—Andy Warhol

Whether Warhol meant that fame would be fleeting or that fame would come to virtually all of us is unclear. What is clear, however, is the wonderful, energizing feeling of people recognizing who we are or what we do.

During my tenure as a sales manager, I wanted the members of my team to be proud of the jobs they were doing and the goals they were achieving, *and* I wanted to make sure that they had the training and support necessary to succeed, demonstrating Attribute 26 of The Ultimate Sales Manager.

Attribute 26: Use uncommon ideas to forward other people's careers.

As a result, among my direct reports, I created something called Fifteen Minutes of Fame.

A LOGICAL PROGRESSION OF THOUGHT

With all that my sales team had to do during the workday to meet their objectives, keep clients happy, and ensure their own income, I wanted to be careful not to add unnecessary policies and procedures that might take their focus and time away from being prepared, professional, and productive. But I did not want them to lose sight of their priorities. I wanted the majority of their focus each day to be on *productive* issues that would increase their sales, customer base, and commission rather than on more time-consuming and less immediately productive ideas.

By asking my people to pursue a logical progression of thought, I wanted them to think about when in the day they would work to accomplish certain tasks. First and foremost, I did (and still do, given the chance) everything I could to dissuade people from thinking that there was a particular time of day that was *better* to make cold calls than another. Since you and I have no idea what is going on in the office around the corner, down the block, or across the country, *anytime* is a good time to cold-call.

I point this out because there are certainly tasks and activities that *do not* fit in the mainstream portion of the selling day, including addressing envelopes, gathering brochures and sell sheets for insertion into a mailer, and searching for leads during prime selling time (8:00 A.M. to 5:00 P.M.).

To ensure that I do not appear to contradict myself, allow me to explain. Cold and warm calling is appropriate at any time of the day, because they must be done when there is a high chance of connecting with a human being. Mailings, lead research, and Internet browsing are *not* confined to an 8-to-5 period. I am a big fan of addressing envelopes while watching *SportsCenter.* I like to look up leads at the end of the day, when I do not feel as though every minute off the phone is a lost opportunity.

There is an old joke, which is only funny because it is true: Guess what burning question is asked, in every sales office, at 9:28 A.M.? "What's for lunch?" Essentially, my philosophy and practice is that just because something comes up (a prospect asks you to mail or e-mail them some information), it does not mean you drop everything to accomplish that task.

NOT TIME MANAGEMENT; ACTIVITY MANAGEMENT

All of us are sometimes distracted by what time management consultants call, "the tyranny of the urgent." This is the all-too-familiar situation where we know what is *important* (and want to do that), but end up doing what is deemed *urgent*. When faced with these situations, we find ourselves at the end of the business day, feeling tired, frustrated, and anxious because we didn't accomplish what we wanted to, or what we felt we *should* have. To have a greater sense of control, and to give my people a straightforward and structured way to prepare for one-on-one meetings with me, I came up with a 15-minute format that was easy to understand, manage, and track.

Here are the key components of Fifteen Minutes of Fame. You ask your people to mark their calendar and attend a consistently scheduled weekly (or nearly that often) meeting between the salesperson and the manager, where the salesperson does most of the talking. They are required to prepare and come to the meeting with the following information:

♦ Hot prospects
♦ Pending deals
♦ Results from the previous week (specifics only)
♦ Expectations for the upcoming week (note that I did not say *goals* for the upcoming week)

This form should be a simple form that you create, to be filled out by each salesperson prior to his or her scheduled one-on-one meeting.

BOTH KNOW WHAT TO EXPECT

Managing expectations is a consistently reliable tool for The Ultimate Sales Manager. If I set a goal for you, and you do not achieve it, you react negatively. If you and I set an expectation together, we agree that the expectation is reasonable to work toward and something to strive for. The Fifteen Minutes of Fame conversation is not designed to soften or replace goal setting. The idea is to create an environment where the salesperson has your undivided attention, so that she can *wow* you. It is her sole time to share with you how she has done her job. Has she gone above and beyond? Has she taken risks? Has she towed the line or expected to be recognized for standard performance? Has she landed a particular client? Fifteen Minutes of Fame is the time to share all of this. It is a window into her personality, as well as a great opportunity for you to learn how she prepares and presents.

Salespeople will want to *wow* you. They are looking for your support, and they really want your approval. Structure these conversations so that they are not rehashes of deals lost or leads not followed up on, but are about the immediate past and the pending future, allowing you to listen and learn. It allows your salespeople to sell you on how reliable and consistent they are. It is really great fun.

You are also affording them an uninterrupted forum in which they can interact with you, one on one. Many of the individuals on your team probably crave this, but heavy workloads and fast paces at which each must accomplish his or her tasks for the day rarely allow for it.

PREEMPTIVE BEHAVIORS

Drop-In Visits

Throughout the day, salespeople will walk into your office and give you detailed descriptions of negotiations in progress and great leads or deals they expect to close. Salespeople use these "drop-in" visits as a vehicle to gain quick approval of what they are doing and to prevent possible micromanagement on your part. They hope to preempt any detailed questions, or questions from you for which they may not be prepared. This allows them to avoid scrutiny.

Halt in the Hallway

Another preemptive technique common to salespeople is what I call the "halt in the hallway." This is when you are on your way somewhere, to do something, and you may be mentally a few miles away. A salesperson sees this as an opportunity to share a litany of details from pending situations, and you halt to listen, and then go on your way. I realized after a few of these interactions that the person who stopped me would rarely be able to provide specific details when asked for them. He or she was hoping to throw details or facts at me without substance, and that I would not be able to keep track because I presumably had *so much on my plate.*

An important distinction between Fifteen Minutes of Fame and other management conversations is that your salespeople fill out the brief, four-point form every week, in advance of this meeting, giving structure and focus to the meeting. They provide you with a copy of the four-point form, which you keep. You maintain a reverse chronological record of the hot prospects, pending deals, and so on. It is a powerful tool that can help put you in the position to inspect what you expect.

When salespeople are asked to focus their reporting and save the good news for Fifteen Minutes of Fame, the impromptu conversations you have with them are less about them trying to impress you and more about ways that you can help them achieve the objectives they set for themselves.

HISTORY OF FIFTEEN MINUTES OF FAME

I created Fifteen Minutes of Fame in response to what many managers had shared with me as a difficult problem—getting details from, tracking activity of, and maintaining accountability with salespeople. I started teaching it, and used it to great effect when I was the general sales manager with Nationwide Cellular. At that time, I had seven locations, 35 salespeople, and seven managers reporting to me.

When I offered the Fifteen Minutes of Fame concept to my managers, they were a bit resistant. They thought they had all the details they needed. As an experiment, I started Fame sessions with salespeople in a few of the locations. After I visited, I would wait a day or two, and then call the manager of the location I had visited, and ask for the status of the deals about which their salespeople had been so excited.

This was an eye-opening experience for some of the managers because they worked within a few feet of some of these salespeople, and I was more in touch with how the salespeople were managing deals and prospects than the local managers were.

When I visited these locations again, people would "halt me in the hallway." Immediately, I started telling them: "Sounds great— bring it to 'Fame'," or "Save it for 'Fame'." I wanted to create a habit, and I wanted my team to share the amazing things they had accomplished in a forum where I was attentive, and could get the details. (We tend to have long memories for certain things, short memories for others.) I wanted them to get their due, as well as satisfy my requirement to be accountable. Keeping good records of whom they called, the status of their potential and current deals, and other details only helped them because they had to speak in specifics.

I then handed the Fame sessions off to their managers. It was a great gift. It did not solve every problem or increase sales 7,000 percent, but it helped the managers to connect with the salespeople; it helped the salespeople because they felt their managers knew how focused they were, and how hard they worked; and it helped my managers update me with the insights and details of deals, which they were aware of after several weeks of Fame sessions.

Directed Reporting

Implementing Fifteen Minutes of Fame allowed me inside the heads of my sales team in a new and unique way. It compartmentalized their thinking and allowed me to offer more specific advice, coaching, and feedback on particular techniques because the 15 minutes was all about them, and the discussion was focused on specific tasks, prospects, and efforts. Salespeople tend to like that. (Who doesn't?)

What came as an unexpected benefit was the ability to see in just a few short weeks, how committed different salespeople were to truly qualifying prospects, detailing their contact records, and negotiating well.

Practical Application

John Lesinski, the managing director for Grubb & Ellis Company for the Baltimore/Washington, DC, region, leads 40 salespeople across three different offices and has one sales manager reporting to him. I was interested in hearing from John, for a few reasons. One, we share a common bond, both having served in the military. In addition, John is the living example of Attribute 27 of The Ultimate Sales Manager.

Attribute 27: Always think two steps ahead.

John applies this when preparing for one-on-one meetings, and I asked him what he expects (and what he gets) out of one-on-one meetings with his people.

JL: When I have one-on-one meetings, I am interested in hearing people talk about their business plans. I want people walking out of one-on-one meetings having accepted a challenge for themselves. I remember someone a few years ago who set a goal that I felt was lower than what she was capable of. It was my challenge and job to have her walk out with a new challenge and without her feeling like she had 16 tons of weight on her chest.

You get people to do well by employing two prime motivators—love and fear. You have to show a level of appreciation, or love, and do what you can realistically to create a sense of fear, if they have not met your expectations. Not a fear of me—I don't agree with that management style. I mean a fear of, or discomfort with, doing less than expected.

I want my people to be continually challenging themselves, and the fear of failure is a great motivator for good salespeople. They are like professional athletes. They know that they are only as good as their last deal. I run a group of people who have to go out and prove themselves every year, and that is what we discuss in our one on ones.

JK: Who in their right mind would be a sales manager?

JL: Leadership junkies. These are people who like to build, accept responsibility, and work with others to achieve a greater goal. The best sales managers may not be motivated by money as much as a feeling of accomplishment motivates them.

Accomplishments must be supported and created by specific, measurable results. By having them report details, you help them clarify what is real and what is hoped for. Salespeople will leave a name on a hot prospect list as long as they possibly can. The downside to this activity is that if the salesperson sees names on their hot list, they assume that they do not need to go out and get some more names for that list. *Wrong*.

A HABIT FOR YOU BECOMES A HABIT FOR YOUR TEAM

The key to success (yours and theirs) in Fifteen Minutes of Fame is *consistency*. Doing it one week, but not the next, is a bad idea. Like many management training mantras, this must be regular and consistent.

Let's look at it from the employee's point of view: Once you and I have a Fifteen Minutes of Fame session, I am required to follow up on what I committed to. When the same thing happens the following week, and then the following, you have taught me that this is important to you. You have also told me that I cannot slide and let it go for this week (or any week in the future).

After the initial resistance has been overcome (by both you and your team), you develop a rhythm. In the best of all possible scenarios, they start to look forward to it. In the worst case scenario, you find that someone who appeared to be getting things done was doing more talking than walking.

Here are some specific, tangible, and measurable results I have experienced as a result of the proper implementation of Fifteen Minutes of Fame:

♦ Salespeople on a weekly basis set consistent, reasonable expectations.
♦ They gained self-confidence by accomplishing what they set out to do.
♦ They understood what priorities they were to focus on.
♦ The hallway and water-cooler conversations become increasingly about skill development and business and less about "the one that got away."
♦ I, as sales manager, am able to make quicker, more informed decisions about who to let go because I have a clear picture of who is (and who isn't) pulling their weight.

As managers, we become an employee's counselor, confidant, and caretaker. Unfortunately, none of these *directly* generates revenue. Our inventory also goes home every night. Managing salespeople truly is a privilege and a uniquely challenging way to make a living and an impact.

We must empathize with people, and make human connections before we can develop their skills and talents. We *must not* allow that to become a substitute for productive conversations, prudent management, and obtaining results.

In Part III, we take what we have offered so far and build on its foundation. We take a rapid-fire journey from goal setting to daily activity management tools to take your team to an amazing new level, this year, next year, and beyond. By now, you have identified with some or all of the concepts offered up to this point. By now, you have decided whether you are, or soon will be, The Ultimate Sales Manager. Now, things get more interesting, because from here on out, it is all about implementation, measurement, motivation, and accomplishment.

PART III

Planning and Preparation

9

GOALS LEAD
TO GREATNESS

I had a pastor once who described certain Saturday nights as his "dark nights of the soul." This was because he was expected to preach the following day, and he was nervous that he would forget a key point, add something that may not be relevant to the point, or just freeze.

These dark nights did not overwhelm him *every* Saturday night, but they occurred and distracted him often enough that he named them. I think that any time you ask a salesperson reporting to you to prepare his goals for the following selling period (week, month, or year), he can be hit by a sudden, unique combination of anxiety and amnesia.

When we are asked to recount our accomplishments, many of us will look blankly into the void, and wonder if we have actually ever accomplished anything. This odd experience manifests itself when we ask people to prepare for Fifteen Minutes of Fame and this is exactly why we give them advance notice of these meetings.

When it is time for you to sit with your folks and prepare commitments to goals, you must take a very avuncular approach. This is not the time to have a photographic memory or to list everything this person has ever hoped for or tried to accomplish, rubbing his nose in how and when he may have fallen short. At the same time, your consistent performers must not be made to feel as if the work and production they have previously delivered is now in the past and as such does not matter.

As with everything The Ultimate Sales Manager does, you must approach this with tact, patience, strength of mind, and a sense of humor. You must also apply Attribute 28 of The Ultimate Sales Manager to all goals conversations.

**Attribute 28: Ensure that the plan
salespeople submit can be accomplished
by that person with the tools at their disposal.**

Setting goals is your folks' opportunity to learn about their sense of what is possible, what is worth working for, and most important, how they can truly change their life. Not too many professions offer people the opportunity to regularly increase their income, based solely on the amount of work, wit, intellect, and desire they are willing to invest.

With goal setting, The Ultimate Sales Manager should be:

♦ Brief but committed
♦ Positive
♦ A leader
♦ Supportive
♦ Realistic

CREATING A COMMUNITY

Robin Mee is the president and founder of Mee, Derby & Company, an executive search firm based in Cabin John, Maryland. She has sold for over 23 years and has managed salespeople for more than 17 years. In a recent conversation with Robin, she touched on a variety of issues, and the thing she was most animated and emphatic about was what role goal setting plays in the overall environment of a sales office. She said:

The most important thing to me is to create a culture that really is a community. I am convinced that people today are looking for something they can connect to, and the workplace offers that unique opportunity. As the manager, you have to create and foster that, through your management style.

It is clear that companies that do not do well are the ones without strong leadership and strong management. Leadership is related to management, but it is not the same thing. John, you mentioned to me before this interview that your definition of "to manage" was *to get the most out of*. I agree with that. In addition, I think that leadership is about taking people to their next level of excellence. It is about goal setting, activity tracking, and measuring against goals set.

Goals should be set by the salesperson, with the manager's guidance and direction. I want them to set their own goals, and I work with my people every month to see where they are in relation to those goals. Salespeople may be reluctant to set goals, but my philosophy or outlook is: "If you don't have a plan, how will you know when you have accomplished anything?"

JK: What are some words that would best define your approach to creating a culture and a sense of community?

RM: Respectful, supportive, driven, communicative, responsive, smart, and intuitive. I want a team who wants feedback. Continuous feedback is essential.

Salespeople are different from sales managers, in that salespeople tend to be more competitive, where as the sales manager wants to win, but through the efforts—the combined efforts—of the team. A good sales manager is a team player, whereas top-performing salespeople may not be. I want to create a positive energy that you can feel when you are in the office. Believe it or not, there are some salespeople who are highly negative, and those people will suck the life right out of your team.

JK: What does The Ultimate Sales Manager always keep in mind?

RM: We have heard people say, "It's not what you say; it's how you say it." I think the vocabulary that you use and choose is so important. A simple formula would be: Vocabulary + Delivery + Exceptional   Listening   Skills = Good Communication.

BE REALISTIC

Goals are a combination of fantasy and reality, of truth and science fiction. And this is exactly what you want them to be. Make sure that you do not limit your discussion of goals to what you need from your people to make your assigned quota.

Find out what achievement would get your folks excited. As we learned earlier, not everyone in sales is money motivated. It is important that it is a key desire for them, but the long-term regular producers do it for the thrill because it is a mental challenge, or because they know that they are doing something that most people do not have the skill, fortitude, or patience for, and most satisfyingly for the long-term folks: They do it well. This is a great time to think about and acquire Attribute 29 of The Ultimate Sales Manager.

Attribute 29: Recognize the unique skills, gifts, fears, and aspirations of each of your salespeople.

Goals set will be different for everyone on the team, yet they are traditionally created in three levels:

1. Long-term goals
2. Medium-term goals
3. Short-term goals

I have no quarrel with these as guidelines, but I think it is important that you, The Ultimate Sales Manager, incorporate a bit more creativity. With the good management practice of knowing your folks' wishes and desires, it is surprisingly effective to be able to bring up in conversation that concert that Susan wants to go to, or to mention in a sales meeting that Phil plans to buy a boat with his next commission check. I also heartily believe that goals need to be tracked, and when *not* achieved, recast immediately.

We do not want our salespeople to have dark nights of the soul. We want them to look at goal setting as a guidepost for their activity. Specific, directed activity has served every professional I have seen or worked with, so I most heartily encourage you to make sure that, regardless of the experience or production level of your individual team members, you hold them to an activity standard.

This selling profession is demanding and unforgiving. It stands in the middle of the room, arms folded, challenging all of us to fight this honorable fight, and win!

Goals are fun when they have a specific, measurable endpoint. The work toward the goal takes on a mind of its own. The Ultimate Sales Manager helps each individual write down goals, encouraging him or her to post them somewhere in plain view.

I encourage people to write out key training concepts, post them on their desk for approximately 10 working days, then move the sign to another spot on their desk or wall for about 5 working days, and then throw that piece of paper away.

Why? Think about the number of signs you see when driving between your home and the local grocery store. How often do you read the street signs? Probably several times the first few days that you lived there, and then a few times when you had to give directions to someone else, and that's it. You no longer read the signs because your mind has stored that information. When you post something on your desk or wall, you read it for a time, then it becomes like wallpaper—nondescript, uninteresting, and it makes no further impression.

I want you to have your folks write out their goals in their own handwriting (not printed off the computer) so that it captures their attention for a longer time. After 10 business days, move it to somewhere else, but it should be somewhere that the salesperson looks regularly. After a five-day period, sit and speak with the salesperson, ask him what has happened in the past few days that he thinks might help him toward his goal.

Over and over again, I have been amazed at how salespeople have become more focused. This has led to eliminating their distractions, and increasing their activity. Salespeople marvel at how all of a sudden, things can be happening on the desk of someone who has spent several days in the office, not socializing, not surfing the Internet, not killing time, but working the phone, staying in contact with people—making stuff happen!

So, avoiding the "dark nights of the soul" is a great feeling, and that is good for the average sales manager. But The Ultimate Sales Manager has higher expectations. The Ultimate Sales Manager wants to have people do, achieve, and enjoy selling in their environment more than anywhere else. Keeping in mind that which a great philosopher once said:

You will never find people to work for you who will work like you.

This truism (sounds like Attribute 23) is called the Hobson Principle. (Hobson is my close friend, Bill Hobson, and he counsels me on a regular basis about what stresses me out.) When I was running a sales team some years ago, I was frustrated that I was always the first one in the office each morning. Worse, I was the first one to start actually working within a reasonable amount of time after arriving at the office.

I have a funny way of looking at things: I think that if you are paying people to work for you, they should eat their breakfast, tie their tie, or finish applying their makeup *before* they arrive! Above and beyond that, I also expect that if you are "at work," this indicates that you are prepared to engage in work-related activities, as opposed to running out 20 minutes after you arrive to get something to eat, buy your premium branded franchised coffee type beverage, or have a smoke. *But* the Hobson Principle was something with which I struggled. I had to bite my tongue when people would come to the office, but not actually start to participate in the workday until al-most an hour into it.

Now, what does this have to do with goal setting? The Ultimate Sales Manager wants as many people as possible on his or her team to exceed any past performance, and although it is true that many of us want our people to have better lives as a result, we have a respon-sibility to our employer to make the goal/budget/plan that has been assigned to us. So, we need to balance human frailty with require-ments and expectations of production.

ANOTHER ATTRIBUTE

This tells us that we must apply and adopt Attribute 30.

Attribute 30: Recognize what your salespeople have in common, and what they do not.

As true as I feel the Hobson Principle is, the reality is that every-one works for himself or herself. People work to support their fam-ily, but the commonly accepted vernacular is that as a sales manager, you have people working *for* you because there must be a chain of command to maintain order. Each organization must have a struc-ture, or you end up with chaos. A parallel may be drawn regarding the concept of a "company" to a military unit—a company is a group of individuals all brought together to achieve a common goal: vic-tory.

Victory for The Ultimate Sales Manager is to win an account away from a competitor. Victory is also having a group of people who are upbeat and productive. Victory is having more people at-tend the winner's circle, presidents' club, or top-performers' event this year than last, thanks to your success in applying these sensible, human techniques.

Since people may work for you but not like you, setting goals is a great way to remove mental clutter for and with your folks, and it helps you in both planning and commitments. The relationship you have with your folks is tenuous, delicate, and even fragile. One misstep can affect your credibility, your ability to inspire and lead, and even your ability to be a mediocre, struggling sales manager, instead of The Ultimate Sales Manager.

The contention of Part III is that "goals lead to greatness." There are few experiences in the professional world that compare with standing next to the person who may have had some personal struggles, who may have strayed off the professional path at some point during the year, or for whom you decided to stay late or provide some latitude, when he or she is accepting an award for top performance. That plaque, trophy, or incentive gift will stay with that person for a long time, and you will be able to be a part of that experience for eternity.

When I had my first book published, it was clear that there was an opportunity for me to leave a legacy beyond my family. What I was reminded of very soon after that was that everyone I had ever managed who had made more money, found more to enjoy in the profession, or even got out of a rut because of something I said or did was an immeasurable legacy.

The Ultimate Sales Manager does not put herself on a level above her people. Sometimes we are caught up, emotional, or angry about the way people act or react on the selling floor and in their interactions with us or, even worse, with customers. Attribute 31 is a reminder that we have to maintain decorum and professionalism.

Attribute 31: Never chastise or berate in public or in private.

THE HIGH ROAD

The Ultimate Sales Manager puts himself in a position to serve and support his people. Leadership theories vary, and management concepts are argued from the mahogany hallways of corporate America to the campuses of academic institutions, but sales management stands alone as a profession and calling that evolves and transforms not only the people who are being managed but also the people who call themselves managers.

Helping salespeople better themselves and take obstacles out of the way of their success is a heady enterprise. It takes humility. It requires the best you have to offer, and the rewards are nearly euphoric. Goals lead to greatness because of the truth in Thomas Edison's words:

If we actually achieved what we were capable of, we would astound ourselves.

The Ultimate Sales Manager wants team members to astound themselves regularly. What a great feeling.

Let's take a look at goals from the perspective of one of the great minds working in sales management today. Phil Jakeway is the president of The Supporting Cast, a specialty staffing service located in New York City. I asked him about the importance, impact, and practice of setting goals. Phil feels that it is very rewarding to be a sales manager because he helps people realize their potential, while they participate in his company realizing its potential.

JK: Phil, what do you like about managing salespeople?

PJ: One of the fun things is that it is an ongoing challenge. I am specifically passionate about goals. I think it is one of the best ways to help salespeople achieve what they are capable of. The goals must be the salespersons' goals. I learned this the hard way, early in my career; I would set my own goals, instead of theirs. For the past dozen years or so, I have made sure that the salespeople set their own goal.

I may have a total dollar goal that I want us all to achieve, but I would rather have salespeople set goals about production week to week and what their commission dollars will come out to be, based on that targeted goal.

If we start with the total dollar goal, and break it down to net margin dollars, it doesn't just talk about dollars sold, it shows the profitability of those goals. It is much more meaningful to each person to see how it affects him or her. I am also very careful to keep my eyes out for a "fudge" factor.

JK: So, they will put out a goal that they can achieve relatively easily?

PJ: Exactly. Part of having salespeople set goals is that you want them to aspire to something that will be challenging. It has to be challenging, otherwise salespeople (consciously or not) will set goals that they know they can do, and get some pats on the back, and you as the manager will not turn up any heat on them. It's also important to realize that you have to set different goals for people with different levels of experience.

JK: So what types of goals do you set with someone with maybe five years of experience in your environment?

PJ: In the staffing industry, salespeople are typically measured by the billing dollars of their accounts on a weekly basis. So, I will sit down with experienced account execs and set a productivity goal for their billing level of between $50,000 to $60,000 per week. Yet, these are productivity goals. It is important to remember that it is *selling activity* that produces these productivity goals.

We need to set activity goals that are specific, measurable, and achievable. My experience has shown that for every 10 qualified prospects where you are moving the conversation forward on a regular weekly basis, you will be able to generate one client presentation. If your activity goal is to make 5 client presentations in a week, you need to successfully complete 50 quality conversations each week to make this happen. Our salespeople set goals for the numbers of quality conversations (voice mails don't count) that they will achieve each week and then we track them in ACT! our contact management system.

A great sales manager is able to keep his sales team focused on their daily and weekly activity goals. When these are achieved, the productivity goals are sure to follow.

AIM HIGH

If you are not shooting for the stars, get out of the way and let someone else lead your team. This is not a "warm and fuzzy, all things being equal" statement, nor is it designed to make you feel good. It is designed to get you off your keyster (rear end) and busy selling goal setting to you team. If you are a goal setter, this chapter will be useful to you because it will refresh and reinforce some things you already know. This is just as valuable as sending a five-year selling veteran to a seminar on cold calling because people forget things, because there may be some new ideas out there that you have not been exposed to. Even if these ideas are not fully in line with your philosophy, there might be a perspective that makes you think. After all, you bought this book, and it makes sense to see how we weave the entire fabric of ideas together.

Goals make a difference. There have been studies, tests, research, and exercises that prove this, yet the results seem to surprise people. I say they "seem" to surprise people, because it has never been proven that people without goals accomplish anywhere near as much as people who do set goals.

If you invest in the stock market, you are aware of the corporate goals of the different companies with which you invest your trust and money. If you follow any organized sports team, you are cognizant of the goals of that team, coach, or program. The interviews and research you read almost always begin a quote with "We know what our challenges are, and our goal is to . . ."

For me, what makes goal setting exciting is how often there are upsets. The underdogs may not always win the big game, but boy, is it exciting to watch them compete. It's exciting because they have something to prove. They want the world—and that world might be the neighborhood or the international media—to watch that particular competitive endeavor.

You have something to prove because before you started reading this book, you were good at something. You have a gift, or collection of gifts, and you may even be part of a small community that effectively combines skill and talent, and gets results. But the thing that you feel compelled to prove at this stage is that *you* are The Ultimate Sales Manager. Throughout the previous parts and chapters, we have discussed The Ultimate Sales Manager as a fictional crea-ture, with whom I had hoped you would identify. Now, I want you to take on that moniker, and charge back into your work, and put goal setting to work for you in some new ways.

NO LIMITS, NO BOUNDARIES

When I told my father about the first commission structure that was described to me, I told him how much I "could" make under that plan. Without missing a beat, Dad said, "Why do you limit yourself to a number?" That hit me like a ton of bricks, and it stayed with me long enough to remember it, 22 years later.

I assign a very high importance to goal setting, and I think that setting goals beyond dollars of income puts flesh on the bones of the goal-setting discipline. When you have your team set goals for something other than dollars closed, you allow them to access a more creative portion of their brain and personality.

I am neither a mystic nor overly superstitious—although I have met and worked with people who used both approaches for attain-ment of their goals. I am a realist (who happens to have a deep faith). So, being balanced in my approach to goal setting, I spoke with people from the staffing industry, the private gym industry, and Todd Katler of Rent.com about goals, their importance, and how to keep people focused on attainment of those goals. I also wanted to hear about what happens when someone does not make his or her goal for a month, or a quarter.

GET PASSIONATE ABOUT GOAL SETTING

My good friend Todd Katler is the director of sales for Rent.com, an *eBay company*. Rent.com is in the business of connecting qualified renters with landlords via the Internet. He runs a team of 20 sales-people, with two managers reporting to him. His team is spread across the United States. After selling for six years, Todd moved into sales management and has been a selling manager for most of the 12 years he has been a sales manager. I asked Todd to share his approach to goal setting:

> TK: There is an executive process to setting goals. First, you have to determine what the business needs are for your company. Then the hard part happens. You might say, "We have a business need, and we have 10 salespeople, so let's give each one of them 10 percent of what is needed."
>
> I am adamantly against that, because I think it is dangerous—you are forcing your people to fit into activity, and things do not happen that way. You could have a quota that is not attainable.
>
> You have to take your business-need number, and then consider your sales team and their realistic output. You need to evaluate the business need against the output and see how close you are to reality. You set goals that are achievable but not so easy that you could squash them. I aim for a very aggressive goal that takes effort, productivity, and leverage to achieve. We have to give the salespeople the income potential to disincentive them to churn, and then say, okay let's multiply that out by 10.
>
> Then, we decide to either give them more support, or take a reality check and realize that we need to add more salespeople. Do we need to increase marketing dollars? Better yet, is our output high enough to reach the business need?
>
> But I am adamantly opposed to simple even division because you are doing wishful thinking. It's like saying I am going to drive 300 miles in three hours. That does not sound too difficult, until you do the math. It means that you have decided to travel at 100 miles per hour, as opposed to being realistic, choosing a speed limit closer to logic and the law, and making an informed decision that informs your plan. You have to think it through. What makes sense? What is reasonable to expect?
>
> You want to know what is a challenging but attainable goal for the salesperson to achieve each day. I know that there will be good weeks and bad weeks. That means that

there will be good months and bad months. I always tell people numbers based on what I know can be done because I have done it.

I have someone who works for me who is profoundly productive, and she makes more calls than any salesperson I have ever worked with, and my boss thinks it is easy to say, "Why don't you just find seven of her?"

You cannot take your one shining star and make that person the standard. That means that he is a shining star, but there are still people looking to rise to the occasion. Our job as managers is to give the salespeople the tools they need to succeed, the support and training they need, and encouragement, but after that, they need to pick up the phone.

My current sales positions are "prospecting heavy." It is an aggressive job because there are a lot of people who think they want to do it, but after they attempt it, they realize how hard it is.

We keep investing in new tools for our salespeople. We have just introduced a program where we will do some prequalifying for our salespeople, with the goal of them not spending time with people to whom our service will not be useful.

JK: So, how do you distribute the total sales goal for the team?

TK: The first thing I do is add up the elements. People sometimes look at their sales strategy as a lot more art than science. The skills required to capture someone's attention and to communicate effectively makes people great at sales, but what often gets missed is the raw numbers required to reach your goals. You need to learn enough about yourself and what it takes to sell what you sell and to know what you need to do each day to reach your numbers.

I emphasize at every opportunity that salespeople need to now how many phone calls they need to make to hit their number. Once they figure that out, the rest is not hard. Salespeople are not overly numbers oriented, unless it comes to their paycheck. They are not overly organized, either. Cold calling and sales in general can be a little frustrating, and people can come up with a million reasons why they should not make a sales call.

To help people plan, we need to help them take their emotions out of it and determine a hard number that reliably tells them what they need to generate to hit that assigned number. If they want to hit the next bonus level, they need to increase that number. Salespeople decide for themselves where they want to sit, in terms of ranking, and income. It's that simple.

I often tell people: "If you can figure out a way to get the same results with less calls, then all the better." Of course, until then, I want them to go the route we have laid out for them.

The title of this chapter is "goals lead to greatness." I believe this with every fiber of my heart, soul, and mind. I do believe that everyone is capable of greatness, and the privilege of managing, coaching, and developing other people (as you and I do) is that we can be instrumental in helping people to identify, aspire to, and achieve a greatness in their lives that they never thought possible.

I talk with many of the people to whom I have sold training about how amazing it feels to see someone start with them at an entry-level or cold-calling position and in a short time, start talking about the home she will buy, or the new car, or the dream vacation she will go on. Or she talks about a great, new snow blower.

The "thing" they acquire or the security they enjoy is not the issue. The issue, and the most foundational reason for guiding and tracking your people through goals, their attainment, and the ultimate rewards, is that you offer them something that no other profession can. They can determine their own income. That, very simply and beautifully, is powerful.

Set goals with your folks. Set goals for your team. While you track and discuss the goals of people on your team, you will soon be able to help them remove obstacles in a way that they never could before. You are about to learn about a simple, elegant formula for having people on your team get a clear idea of what they need to do, and what they need to stop doing, to achieve the goals that you and they have agreed are reasonable, attainable, and maybe just a bit difficult. I tell my children: Very few things worth doing are easy.

Aspiring to, reaching for, and even thinking that you might be able to attain greatness in this amazing profession is honorable, and I heartily encourage it. Be a hero. Be unique. Be daring.

10

THE THREE-STEP BUSINESS PLAN

LEADERSHIP IS VISIBLE, RELIABLE, AND MEMORABLE

Attribute 32: Inspect what you expect.

You, The Ultimate Sales Manager, need to demonstrate the traits of efficiency and focus you want your salespeople to emulate. Your ethics and morale, and the culture that you create, are a large contributing factor in how your team members conduct themselves, interact with each other, and respond to you. Positive or negative, your actions are going to be emulated. As such, it is essential to be aware that what you say, and how you say it, influences the people reporting to you.

When I was a sales trainer at a vitamin company in Southern California, my colleague Melbia would say to me, *"If it's on your mind, it's on your face."* Her point was that I was not particularly adept at hiding how I felt about people, their actions, or their reactions to how I dealt with them.

Earlier, when we heard from Dennis Napoliello, he shared some gathered wisdom. Let's make that statement Attribute 33.

Attribute 33: Know that you will be the topic of someone's dinner conversation.

Your words and actions will continue to influence those around you long after they are said or done.

P + P = P

The task of managing salespeople brings with it a huge learning curve, which may last 30 years. The Ultimate Sales Manager is a work in progress. It is not a job, but rather a large-form art project.

If you thought about writing a novel, or an opera, you would have to think about the arc of your story—the pieces that hold up the overall larger work assumptions (i.e., cultural truths, linguistic nuance, and relevancy to the listener or reader)—and the same is true of your sales management career. Pursuing a career in sales management is one of the most creatively demanding things you can do with your professional life.

Working Creatively

To effectively build meeting agendas over and over, to deliver relevant advice and instruction to the same audience, and to keep it sounding fresh and personalized requires tremendous creativity. The purpose of the Three-Step Business Plan is to take that creativity and funnel it into something that will help you and your folks be prepared, professional, and productive.

Mechanics and Nuance

The Three-Step Business Plan is meant to be used as a quarterly exercise, but should not become a cumbersome or restrictive part of your team's tasks. It should help inform your Fifteen Minutes of Fame conversations and prepare you for what will be explained in Chapter 11.

The mechanics of creating and documenting the details of the Three-Step Business Plan are designed to be straightforward and concrete, and thus recorded on paper. The nuance is in how you and your salespeople utilize the information and the tracking ability you obtain through utilizing the Three-Step Business Plan as a historical document for each production quarter.

Reasonable Expectations

As a sales manager, you are responsible for setting the tone of the environment and level of compliance of your team, on a person-to-person basis. In your relationship with your sales team, there are certain things that they are going to expect from you (e.g., recognition, feedback, support, encouragement, answers, or higher commissions). It is only right (notice that I did not say *fair*) that you will want (and expect and receive) certain things in exchange. You expect employees to be accountable for their time, both in and out of the office. Salespeople expect to be paid on time and correctly. They also expect you to help them make even more money, so it is only right that you expect them to provide you with a written plan.

I have managed sales teams where there would be one person who was of the opinion that the current, stated, specific rules and expectations did not apply to him because he was so productive. Issues would arise and conversations would become contentious with him because he did not perform according to my other criteria: being prepared and professional. The Three-Step Business Plan eliminates excuses. It takes a no-nonsense, unforgiving, no-excuses-will-move-me approach.

Three ideas or areas of concern for you, and everyone reporting to you, are:

1. Targets
2. Tactics
3. Time

You have a tremendous amount of time at your disposal and you probably don't even realize it. Time is a magical thing that marches, moves, measures, and motivates. Time is unforgiving. It does not care if you were planning on accomplishing something, calling someone, or helping someone *later*. Time is only concerned with the here and now. The great cosmic question that you must examine (and have your folks examine) is what you are doing with the most immediate and precious resource at your disposal—this inimitable, immeasurable, relentlessly consistent thing that we refer to as time.

THE POWER OF NOW

The mind-set regarding time for individuals living in the United States is unique in the world, and in my opinion, very much to our detriment. There are ambitious societies, and strong global economic powerhouses, besides the United States, yet there are none that I have experienced firsthand who place such a low premium on the *now* as we do.

Traveling the world as part of the world's finest navy, and then taking many business and pleasure trips across continents and oceans has given me the perspective (and the confidence) to bring this issue up in this context. *Now* is a fleeting thing, and as someone who grew up in the United States, I always found it fascinating how several cultures around the world slow down or stop working completely at midday. We take time and beat it to death with our expectations and demands, as opposed to cherishing it for the rarity that it is and making the healthiest use of it that we can.

Many countries throughout Europe have a different work attitude, but it is clear that there is a large emphasis on time off from work throughout the European Union. Here in America, people are shocked if they hear of a friend taking more than two entire weeks off from work in a row, expecting to have their job waiting for them when they return. This is ludicrous to the European mind-set, and if you visit there, you will see people living less stressful, more family- and recreation-focused lives.

So, what does that tirade have to do with the venerable topic of this chapter? Only everything, because the moment-to-moment choices we make add up to a lifetime in the blink of an eye. If I choose to be prepared and professional, I can be productive without working myself to death.

THIS IS FUN

If you want your sales team to enjoy what they do, you must demonstrate and discuss the joy you find in the work that *you* do. This can only be beneficial to your team's mental health, and production levels. If they are happily closing business, they are making more money, you are meeting your boss's (or your shareholders') expectations, and all is right with the world. If time is so precious, and you do not want to kill it, you must plan as if you know that it is coming. My wife is fond of asking me at different stages of the year (and at 4:00 P.M. on Friday): "What do you want to eat tonight for dinner?" I look at her and say, "I make decisions all day at work. And, you know what we have in the house—what are our choices?"

She retorts with, "Well, I didn't plan anything." The first 100 times we went through this routine, I asked, "Didn't you assume that Friday was coming again and that we might want to eat dinner?" I was very careful to keep sarcasm out of the mix—sarcasm rarely serves the marital conversation, and to prove it, I can tell you how comfortable our living-room couch is to sleep on. But the point is, we must plan (prepare) so that we respect the power of what we do (professional) so that we can be . . . productive.

REASONABLE, AGGRESSIVE PLANNING

Having someone tell you that she is going to make 50 cold calls a week is a beautiful thing, but how realistic is it, in your environment, and with the tools at the disposal of your team? Phil Jakeway, quoted in Chapter 9, spoke eloquently about realistic, attainable, and most important, specific, measurable goals.

To me, this means that I ultimately have control over what I do within certain allowances or "packets" of time. When people tell me that they don't have time for something, my impression is that that issue or activity is not a high priority for them. Priorities have a way of making themselves known, simply by how they are responded to by each person. I believe that *time* has a way of making you bend to its will.

The clock will not move more quickly or more slowly because you desire it. As such, I have to plan weeks or months in advance to accomplish large projects and tasks. When I have a large target list, I have to be both practical and aggressive to keep myself interested, as well as create urgency in my own mind and plan to complete those tasks.

THE MECHANICS OF THE THREE-STEP BUSINESS PLAN

The Three-Step Business Plan should be written on one sheet of paper, with three specific headings:

1. Targets
2. Tactics
3. Time

When the members of your team present their Three-Step Business Plan to you, all three indicators must be equally represented, respected, and researched. Your job as manager is to walk each salesperson through how to do this so that he or she is clear about what to work toward and how to get there. When we break things down to this simple formula, we focus on the targets, tactics, and time.

Targets

This means that your folks will learn and master the art of qualifying prospects. This means that the people they call on will meet specific criteria that are clear and distinct. The salesperson does not get emotionally involved in various conversations hoping to close a deal with someone, as much as they are trying to figure out how to move the conversation forward. The targets that you and the salespeople agree should be on their list are prospects who fit into the criteria you set or who have yet to be contacted.

Tactics

This refers to the specific activity goals we spoke about in Chapter 9. What specific activities (e.g., calls, visits, or mailings) will this person engage in over the three months following submission of this plan? When the three months are up, you and the salespeople sit and review what was planned and what was achieved. You adjust their next plan accordingly, and everyone knows what is expected of them. It is about removing the mystery of what a salesperson does day to day.

Time

- ◆ "Time marches on."
- ◆ "Time waits for no one."
- ◆ "Time will come today."

Okay, enough of the 1970s pop-song references—time will continue, regardless of whether you recognize it or respond to it. It will not slow down to accommodate your needs. This does not mean that it should be your enemy. It means that when it is time to engage in a substantive conversation with your people about their goals, about where they want to take their income and their achievements, their commitment of time has to be attached to the tactics to which they commit.

Adhering to this plan has been a huge help to sales managers with whom I have consulted, and to me, because it removes all of the fluff in a salesperson's quarterly plan. It points to the three things that add up to increasing and maintaining consistent sales.

It will assist you in determining where in your Three-Tiered Sales Team each person fits because numbers do not lie and because you inspect what you expect. When you maintain a file of the Fifteen Minutes of Fame sheets, and quarterly include the Three-Step Business Plan that each of your people writes and submits, you will know (beyond your gut) who your performers are, who should get more attention, and *who should go*. I find this tool invaluable, and hope that some version of this finds its way into your quest to becoming The Ultimate Sales Manager.

In Chapter 11, we are going to explore a simple, reliable planning tool, called Ten Tasks Today™, that will revolutionize the way your people manage their day.

11

TEN TASKS TODAY

This chapter helps you better equip (prepare) your people with simple, reliable processes that will help keep them productive. Every business day will bring surprises and distractions. Deals will fall through, customers will want refunds or discounts, vendors will have trouble delivering on promises, and more. If you have been in sales, business, or any level of management for more than five days, this looks typical. Yet, what is atypical is how people prepare for all of these potential occurrences.

There are some things you can do to help yourself be prepared and able to anticipate how your day will go. At the end of an ideal business day, consistently productive salespeople spend a few minutes thinking about what they want to accomplish on the *next* business day.

A productive day does not necessarily mean that a deal has closed. It means that there have been conversations or relationships that moved forward, that a significant amount of letters or brochures were put in the mail, or that a handful of tangible, specific things happened that put a smile on both the face of the sales manager and the salesperson.

Days will disappear fast, if you are reactive. Your salespeople may get stuck dealing with nonsales related issues (billing, technical service or support, or even an unsatisfied customer). By nonsales, I mean that in the eye of many salespeople anything that does not directly relate to a commission check.

Even if you run through a day that has a certain amount of thunder and rush, you can identify regular occurrences. Without sounding as if I have a crystal ball, I can confidently say that I have a good idea of what each sales day will hold. A *good idea*— not a carved-in-stone picture. If I know certain things must be done to reach my goals, it follows that the most reliable way for me to accomplish those goals is through discipline and faith. Discipline is doing what must be done, and doing it regularly. Discipline keeps me working through each task to its completion. Faith tells me that incremental steps will result in something significant in the future. By faith, I mean that I have faith that the doors to the office will be open, the phones will be working, and the business world will be in full gear by the time I arrive at my desk. Faith and discipline go hand in hand, and they need each other to survive.

NOT ROCKET SCIENCE

I plan my day in the following way:

- ♦ Each night, to prepare for the following workday, I write out important things I need to remember on my Ten Tasks Today sheet. This sheet is separate from everything else I have in front of me each day, because the sheet is part of a pad that sits in a pocket at the back of the calendar book that I carry.
- ♦ I date the sheets as I use them. Last night, I wrote today's date on the sheet. I reference this sheet all day, and then at the end of the day, I compare the plan with the actual attainment. I then move anything that must be forwarded to the next day.

♦ At the top of each sheet of paper, I write the word: Goals. Next to it, I write three specific, time-sensitive short-term goals that are on my mind, working their way into my subconscious. These are things that I would be very excited to achieve, and I make a point of working toward them each day, in whatever incremental fashion I can. My goals should be reasonable, trackable, not so easy to attain that they do not actually require effort. They should have personal meaning for me.

♦ Many times, I set a quarterly revenue goal, and I rewrite that goal on each Ten Tasks Today sheet that I create. I keep it with my daily calendar, as a reminder, and as a record of what I am working toward. I keep a file of these sheets that goes back about two years. Keeping them on record allows me to refer back to them, gain perspective, and remember past accomplishments. I find this very motivating, because in general, most people tend to underestimate themselves, and find ways for great things *not* to happen. I would rather you create the positive environment we have been discussing, and that can be achieved (in part) by your adopting Attribute 34.

Attribute 34: Understand what motivates your people, and why they choose specific goals.

Each of the salespeople on your team has a perspective on what they are capable of accomplishing, and so do you. As The Ultimate Sales Manager, you must temper your hope with reality and combine motivation with a sense of what is realistic. You also regularly remind yourself of Attribute 35.

Attribute 35: Never assume that what you think people are capable of is the same thing they think they are capable of.

Following the Goals category on my Ten Tasks Today sheet is the next category: Tasks—the actual pieces of work that I want to accomplish that day. I write them in short detail, and put a small circle to the left of each.

When I start a project but get interrupted, or must wait for another resource before I can finish it, I draw a single line through the circle. This tells me I must return to this task. When I complete the task, I draw a horizontal line all the way through my writing, to indicate that it is done, and I no longer need to worry about it.

Sometimes, my typical day is to make 40 calls or to complete some invoicing. Other times, it involves making travel plans for the next series of client visits and seminars that I will conduct. Sometimes, it includes the fact that I have to go to one of my children's swim meets. Still other times it will be to write a new article.

I *never* write more than 10 tasks on any given day. Never is a pretty strong word, especially to an overly optimistic, type-A, over-achieving dreamer like me. But that *never* was learned through experiences called disappointment and disillusionment. I often tell my son: "Experience may not be the most *patient* teacher, but it's the most effective."

LIMIT YOUR LIST

In my experience, regardless of the length of time it might take to complete any individual task (some take half an hour, others just a few minutes), the sum total of the day (any business day) will rarely afford me enough time to complete more than 10 tasks. I am not sure why, but it seems to be a consistent trend.

When you lay out 10 tasks to complete in a given day, you are creating a busy day. You cannot plan every interaction, conversation, or unplanned event, so the beauty of the 10-tasks theory is that you are given room to actually think during your workday. Imagine how useful that would be.

My experience has been that putting down more than 10 tasks works against your goal of being productive because you tend to rush through important tasks to get to the next one (regardless of it's comparative importance). You will lose focus because you have so many things that you think you should get done that day.

I have found (through trial and *multiple error*) that putting more than 10 tasks on a list for a single business day consistently sets me up for disappointment, or worse, failure. I have yet to accomplish more than 10 tasks in any given day with proficiency and aplomb. I would rather limit my list, pay full attention to that list, and possibly give myself a few minutes off at the end of a day than try to be a superman.

YOUR SALESPEOPLE NEED THIS

Salespeople are looking to get a lot done, in a short amount of time, with the least possible demand on their time or effort. This tool will help to further document how the mind of each salesperson works, what he is capable of, or how easily he is distracted from the tasks he sets out to accomplish. It is not the Ten Tasks Today form itself, or the concept that will make him more productive, it is the fact that you will be explaining, inspecting, and reiterating the importance of both the exercise and his ability to complete it.

Your salespeople are amazing creations of nature. They will bring you some of the funniest stories, frustrate you in ways you never imagined, and inadvertently provide you with some of the most rewarding moments of your entire professional life. It is up to you to help them stay on course, stay grounded, and keep running at light speed.

You may get caught up in someone's potential or get frustrated that they never seem to make the final connection between activity, comportment, and drive. This transaction is what leads to the closed deal, and just because you think they can do it, does not mean they can. You cannot want it for them.

PRACTICE MAKES PREPARED

Practice does not make perfect. I have practiced playing the drums for many, many, years, and I am far from the perfect player. Practice makes you prepared because you remove some of the unknowns or intangibles of a selling day by planning your Ten Tasks Today list.

SUPER SUNDAY

Each week, as a regular discipline, I sit with the calendar book I mentioned earlier, for about an hour. I am an old-fashioned man in that I write things down, as opposed to typing them into a PDA. Not to knock the power or facility of the technology or those who use it—I have operated in both theaters. I have owned handheld technological miracles, and, in my personal experience, I have found that using a piece of paper and a pen is still a great way to work out ideas. I can look at what I have written without going through menus. Best of all, paper and pen never crash.

Each Sunday night, I sit with my planner and contemplate the week ahead. In this five-inch by eight-inch wonder, I keep my calendar and a pad at the back to make my Ten Tasks Today list. The most important list of the week, however, is the one I make on Sunday night. Over my years of being in sales, sales management, and as an entrepreneur, I have marveled at other people's ability to waste time. I am not a proponent of the fact that we should be running, working, and pounding away during every waking moment. I appreciate and value rest and relaxation. It is just that during the prime time to be productive during the workweek, I have seen, heard, and had to wait for people while they literally throw time out the window.

CALLS

Every salesperson has calls that he or she needs to make every day. My mantra for the people who would spend a lot of time in the office has always been, "When you are off the phone, you are unemployed." Knowing who to call, and for what reason, and planning it in advance is a great planning exercise for salespeople. It allows them to think through their day in advance and to plan to call more people than they might have without planning.

When people sit at their desk, and stare at the phone or computer, they can freeze. This can easily be avoided by having enough calls planned to make the individual names and addresses of prospects look as though they are part of a larger process.

FOCUS, FOCUS, FOCUS

When I ask you to dial three prospects, each call on that very short list has a high potential to appear intimidating, because if it does not go well with one or two, the entire exercise feels like a failure. If I present you with a list of 50 to call, and ask you to come back to me after the total list has been called, then each one is part of the larger scheme.

It has been my experience (as recently as three weeks ago) that when I ask someone who I am coaching to take on the larger task, he is not afraid to pick up the phone, strictly because of the numbers involved. He can relax, and not put so much stock in *every dial.* With the short list, his mind can prevent him from dialing because he can't think of any reason why anyone would ever buy anything from him.

I would much rather have salespeople start their Ten Tasks Today list with somewhere between 12 and 30 calls written down, so that they can push through the distractions or hesitation and begin their calling.

Each day comes at you with plenty of warning. Helping your salespeople prepare to take command of the day, invest their time wisely, and get the most out of their efforts, is the ultimate accomplishment of The Ultimate Sales Manager.

In Part IV, I share what I believe to be the key skills that every sales manager must master, running the gamut from cold calling to developing presentation skills, from closing to expectation management.

PART IV

Skills All Salespeople Should Have

12

COLD CALLING

Newton's first law of motion (an object at rest tends to stay at rest, and an object in motion tends to stay in motion) also applies to salespeople. Being able to successfully initiate new relationships is one of the most important skills salespeople must master if they are to grow their revenue and help you meet the expectations of your management team, shareholders, or partners. If they become accustomed to cold calling, the cold-calling "object" is in motion. The Ultimate Sales Manager expects her team to regularly set successful conversations in motion.

In sales, having a successful conversation means being able to accomplish several tasks in a very short period. Sometimes that means gathering accurate information while concentrating on the conversations. Other times, it means making an introduction while listening to and writing down the name of the person who answered the phone. Many salespeople struggle with cold calling because they expect to close a deal after one call or one meeting with a prospect. This is unrealistic.

The Ultimate Sales Manager gives her people useful recommendations and reasonable expectations. If salespeople are going to spend time cold calling on a particular calendar day, it is the responsibility of the sales manager (that's you) to help them be prepared. This allows you to be credible, because you live according to Attribute 36.

**Attribute 36: Maintain actions
consistent with your character.**

Cold calling is the most thrilling and intimidating thing to do as a professional seller. If our goal is to increase sales and balance lives (be The Ultimate Sales Manager), it is up to us to take some of the mystery out of cold calling for our team.

DO NOT LET REJECTION DETER YOU

This is very different from "Don't take no for an answer." That archaic philosophy is part of the unfortunate reputation that sales has with the general buying public. It is one thing to have someone knocking on the front door of your home on a Saturday afternoon, who has not sold anything all day, and who just keeps pitching regardless of what you say. It is quite another to be in a professional environment and have someone pushing and pushing to attempt to convince you to buy something.

Business to business selling is a very different environment from consumer sales, in that decision makers (or the people in the position to approve of the purchase) are, in the most general sense, more pragmatic and potentially less fickle than a consumer. Consumers are wary of manipulative salespeople. During the course of a sales call, the thought process of business decision makers typically progresses from evaluating the salesperson's technique to negotiating the parameters of the deal to comparing the vendor to someone from whom they currently buy.

Salespeople are inevitably going to be turned away by prospects. The reasons they get turned away range from things as uncontrollable as the decision maker has come to work in a bad mood that day to noncompetitive pricing in the eyes of the decision maker to just simply bad timing. It could even (and often does) boil down to the simple fact that the salesperson just does not connect on a basic, emotional level with the decision maker.

PLAN TO LISTEN

The Ultimate Sales Manager talks to, and listens to, his folks and tries to find reasonable common ground on which to deal with each of his salespeople.

Attribute 37: Be a great listener.

When you listen, and listen well, people tend to be more comfortable with you. They trust you more readily. By being a great listener, The Ultimate Sales Manager applies and demonstrates a skill and an expectation that the salesperson understands. Specifically, that people will:

1. Buy because they feel that it is a good idea.
2. Buy more from someone with whom they feel comfortable.
3. Buy from someone whom they feel they can trust.
4. Buy from someone who puts them at ease and does not only talk about the sale or the product.
5. Rarely buy from someone whom they have just met.

These five tips are also great to remember when cold calling. Relax, and take from it what you can.

I have had multiple conversations with various sales managers about how certain members of their team get frustrated or deterred after just a few calls. Many times, it is because the sales manager has not properly prepared his team for what they might face.

Cold calling is inherently de-motivating. It can suck the life right out of you! You get up, go out (or pick up the phone), and you are attempting to create a relationship on purpose. Think about the relationships that are most comfortable to you. They probably started informally or as a happenstance. Then think about people whom you were either forced to get to know, or vice versa. These relationships are rarely as important or satisfying as those that happen spontaneously. Yet, the salesperson must find a way to *get to it, get through it, and most important: Do it.*

It is essential that salespeople have reasonable expectations when cold calling, including:

♦ Find a way to leave a positive impression—measure and enjoy the minor successes.
♦ Be invited to a future conversation.
♦ Have someone new hear their name or the name of their company.
♦ Leave the call with *any* new information.

THE KEY TO COLD CALLING

I have cold-called for many years, and I enjoy it. I also follow Attribute 38 of The Ultimate Sales Manager when needed.

Attribute 38: Have the confidence and ability at any time to pick up the phone or walk into a building and make a cold call in front of your folks.

When you can demonstrate the confidence and skill to cold call at a moment's notice, you make it something to which the key people in your group will aspire. I used to love doing cold calling with my team, because it took the pressure off them, and it showed them that I had a right to be their manager, because I was adept at the most difficult thing they would be asked to do.

Cold calling usually does not work when it is not approached properly. You talk about, demonstrate, and expect the team to be prepared, professional, and productive, and cold calling is certainly an important activity to which you should apply these concepts.

By being prepared to cold call, I expect salespeople to:

♦ Do their research before the dedicated time to be on the phone or in the field. The Internet is a beautiful thing. It can provide key information. I use it to get a company's phone number, and to ensure that it is in an industry that might be able to use my Gigabats. *And that is all.* It is very tempting (distracting) to read, explore, and investigate a company's web site. It is also a great excuse not to be on the phone, asking questions, making introductions, and *selling.*

♦ Make sure that your people have one or two generic questions prepared prior to their calling cycle so that they can initiate conversations.

♦ My final expectation for salespeople when they are cold calling is that they are emotionally prepared for something positive. Selling is honorable, demanding, hard, and fun.

What to Say

The best way to prepare for cold calls is to have a structured introduction. After salespeople use this introduction, anything can happen. The conversation can shut down or go off on tangents. My mind-set for cold calling is that I have no idea what is going on in the company I am preparing to call until I actually get the company on the phone. Then, I have fun getting to know people, getting them to talk to me, and getting them to invite me back for a future conversation.

Here are the most basic things you should do, and teach to your salespeople:

♦ Identify yourself (Hi—My name is . . .).
♦ Identify your company (and I am with a company called . . .).
♦ State your reason for the call (and I came in/called today to introduce what we do to the best person there . . .).
♦ Ask an open-ended question. (Who would you suggest I speak to?)

Take the mystery out of it, by facing it outright. Take people of different levels of experience out to different companies and see how you do together.

Cold calling is the foundational criteria for someone to be able to call themselves a professional salesperson, and you as The Ultimate Sales Manager must be as good at it as your top performers. The professional racecar driver can get behind the wheel of any vehicle and make it perform. He doesn't need a specific track, or perfect weather. Professional sellers (strong cold callers) were not born as cold-calling experts. They earned the skill and developed the nerve over time, through experience.

JOIN OUR CLUB

I am proud of my ability to cold call. Not only because it makes me part of an elite club, but because regardless of what you sell, I can come into your company, sit down with a price list, names and phone numbers of prospects, and I can cold call anyone you put in front of me. That strength, that skill, has provided me a way of making a living for over 22 years, and I treasure that ability.

Show your salespeople how they can utilize cold calling to increase their performance. Take them out cold calling. Remove the mystery, and make a unique connection with them as individuals as a result. You will spend much of your time encouraging, cajoling, and inspiring your people to cold-call well. The next step has even more variables, and can be almost as demanding. I say almost because when we address presentation skills in Chapter 13, you may see some examples of unique experiences you have had either while presenting or while watching one of your folks do so.

◆

In Chapter 13, we take presentation skills and examine them through a unique lens.

13

PRESENTATION SKILLS

The Ultimate Sales Manager makes a consistent investment in developing skills and talent among the team. One of the most difficult things to develop is presentation skills. If a salesperson is reluctant to practice a presentation in front of you or your team, it is cause for concern. You should be skeptical about how comfortable the salesperson will be, when it is showtime.

I speak around the world on how to improve sales performance for a living. When I speak to salespeople and sales managers, they ask how I developed the ability to hold an audience's attention. My answer: Start with the basics, practice, get evaluated by someone who is more adept and more experienced at presenting than you are, practice some more, and then spend some more time practicing. Practice in private and in front of groups. I continue to make a living at selling because, after 18 years, I still practice, prepare, and practice some more.

◆

This chapter takes you through what I find to be a reliable approach to presentation skills. Being able to deliver a powerful and compelling presentation is essential because you and your salespeople can lose credibility, opportunities, and worst of all, *deals* because you did not prepare and practice in advance.

RIGID FLEXIBILITY

Ed Friedman spent a portion of his professional career teaching presentation skills to executives around the world. He told me:

> We cannot hire people to be automatons. Because people receive and process information uniquely, we cannot ask that people standardize how they present. Whether they are presenting across the table, or to multiple decision makers, everyone needs to be aware of what good (and great) presentations require.

Comedian Jerry Seinfeld pointed out that speaking in front of groups is the number one fear in America. He said that dying was listed as the number two fear. His "it is only funny because it's true" punch line was: "That means that people at a funeral would rather be in the casket than delivering the eulogy!"

Presentation skills are difficult to master, and the reality of most people's discomfort with presenting tells me that the only way to master it is to face it head on. These skills can be learned, and you and your team must place these skills near the top of your priority list: being able to read, respond to, and control your audience, regardless of its size.

Over many years, I have led teams, built teams, and most important, spoken in front of groups of people who did not report to me. I have learned that every group of people tends to contain the same general cast of characters:

- ◆ The Know-It-All Person
  —To this person, nothing you say is revelatory, new, or particularly inspiring.
- ◆ The Comic
  —Sometimes the Know-It-All and the Comic are one in the same, yet often it is a different personality driving the need to be the one making the joke in the room. Too often, the joke is at your expense. If this makes you think that the person I am describing must be immature, I agree. There is

no "maturity license" for people in business, but this is probably not news to you.

♦ The Yeah-But-What-About Person

—When you are leading a meeting, conducting a training session, or presenting with one of your salespeople in front of an audience, there will almost without fail be a naysayer, a doubter, or someone who needs to show how much smarter he is than you (or anyone else in the room).

♦ The Get-Up-and-Walk-Around Person

—Most meetings will have refreshments, and there will invariably be someone who has no qualms about getting up in the middle of your presentation to investigate, pour, or devour food and drink during your presentation. If this person works for you, it is wise to speak to him about group dynamics and how his disregard for the engagement you are working toward is disruptive. I have had many of these conversations with people who walk around, get up, and lean against the wall, and so on, whilst I conducted meetings or delivered training. Many times the person retorts, "It's not about you; I just wanted something to drink," as if I had accused him of a heinous crime. The issue, which I have explained many times, is that I do not see this action as being about the presenter. It is about the person who walks around; he must demonstrate how he is not bound by rules or expectations that obviously apply to others.

If this is reading like a rant, that is okay with me. This is something that I am passionate about, and in order for you to develop both your own presentation skills, and those of your team, these dynamics must be brought to the fore.

If you do not want people walking around during the meeting, mention something about it at the outset. Someone getting up and walking out of the room, accepting a call on a cell phone, or—worst of all—creating a separate conversation with someone else in the room—is:

- ◆ Rude
- ◆ Unprofessional
- ◆ Unacceptable

Here's the challenge: Over time, you are going to face all of these meeting menaces, and you are going to have to deal with them in different ways. If you are not naturally funny, and are not confident that you can deliver a response to the Comic, it is essential that you prepare differently for meetings where a Comic could potentially distract the audience or call into question your abilities or technique.

YOU ARE ALWAYS PRESENTING

There are aspects of presenting which apply to sales meetings, and vice versa. How you conduct a meeting is a demonstration of your presentation technique, as well as expectations you have for promptness, attendance, and participation. You must be prepared to set the tone of your meetings, and decide what type of atmosphere you want to foster. Quagga's gong may be something to which your folks will respond. However, it may not fit the personality of your team, for whatever reason.

You must, as we discussed regarding hiring, decide *in advance* what type of environment, feel, personality, mood, and overall atmosphere you want your people working in every day. During meetings, trainings, vendor presentations, and, above all, presentations made to prospects, the overall atmosphere is established early, fought over through the presentation, and specifically remembered after the fact by everyone in the room.

I could never have made a living for the last several years as a speaker and sales trainer had I not been sensitive to these issues and had a plan for dealing with them. Good presentations rely on the presenter's ability to engage an audience, communicate a specific message, and get out of the audience's way once the objective of the presentation has been achieved.

This brings us back to the starting point, which is: *You must be aware of what you want your audience to learn from your presentation, and be prepared to deliver it.*

Here are my goals, each time I present, whether the presentation is part of an ongoing sales conversation or I am speaking at a national convention:

- ◆ Have them enjoy themselves (make them laugh).
- ◆ Have them hear something they have never heard before. (As much as people refer to my profession as a "speaker," the speaking I do is the result of a tremendous amount of writing. I write all of the material I present in advance. Then, I rehearse. Then I edit and rewrite.)

THE MUSICAL THREAD

When you prepare, and then present, you are using various aspects of language that have many commonalities with the way music is performed. As a lifelong musician, the concepts taught in speech class and what I learned in music harmony in 10th grade enjoy surprisingly parallels:

Dynamics
Harmony
Silence
Crescendo
Rhythm
Tone
Tempo
Improvisation
Audience response
Emotion
Technique

When you have the nerve to ask a group of adults to sit and listen while you speak, you are *required* to make it a positive experience for them. In the same way that Scott Knorp spoke of having respect and high value for salespeople's time during sales meetings, each presentation is a demand on your audience's time, patience, good will, and the long-term relationship you will enjoy. Let's walk through how each of these musical terms applies to presentation skills.

Dynamics

My drum teacher *told* me about dynamics, but I began to understand the *power* of dynamics (in speech and music) in church. I was raised Roman Catholic and the priest who lead mass on Sundays when I was a preteenager understood the power of, and had mastered the implementation of, dynamics in every sermon he gave.

He would bellow and pause. He would almost whisper and use his hands to tap out rhythmic emphasis on the lectern. He would tell a story that would make the adults (and the children who were paying attention) laugh, and he knew exactly when the laughter was about to die down. He would then deliver a striking, staccato sentence that invariably would be the point, the call to action, the conviction of the day's sermon. It was a joy to watch because he was *really good*.

The dynamics revealed themselves in how he employed different levels of volume. The way he changed it, and how he used it to drive his point, engage his audience, and make you remember what he said is a skill that I employ to great effect today, almost 30 years later. The environment is different, but the goal is the same. To use the original musical instrument, the human voice, to its greatest effectiveness.

Harmony

It is important to be in harmony with the people to whom you are presenting. One privilege I have had is teaching the alumni membership sales staff at UCLA. These are college students, who volunteer to sell memberships in the Alumni Association on campus to people who are thinking more about this weekend's social activities, than about how useful it will be to maintain alumni relationships 10 years down the road.

These folks are a generation my junior, yet I go there because of a family connection with UCLA Medical Center, and because it is a regular challenge for me to make jokes, and use references when teaching basic selling techniques to folks who may not consider selling as the first thing they want to do after graduation.

I have to create harmony. If the group is used to professors who have open discussion classrooms, my high-speed delivery of content may not help us connect. If they want to just learn about the commission structure, then I have to hold their attention with humor that *they* will find funny. I have to tie the presentation in a logical, realistic bow for them, and that is how we have a harmonious experience.

Silence

I love silence. *I love it.* It is the great equalizer. It is a negotiation tool, an invitation, a challenge to bear arms, and an act of supplication. Odd that someone who draws great pleasure from playing the loudest instrument in the orchestra or band revels in silence, but I do. It stops people in their mental tracks. It makes grown women giggle. It makes burly men squirm, and it makes you and I live in a floating, liquid time and space that should feel like freedom but in actuality weighs on us like a concrete slab laid carefully on our chests.

Silence makes you wonder. It puts you in the position of wondering what you should do next, and what the other person (or people) might do next. Silence has been a dutiful and reliable friend to the top composers, musicians, and conductors of all time, and it needs to be something you are in command of when making presentations.

The priest at my church knew how to use silence. He held it by the throat. He owned it. As a result, everyone in church was paying attention when he would break the silence and resume his sermon.

Crescendo

A crescendo typically happens in movie soundtracks, in arguments, and in the best presentations. You can tell where it is going, and you are thrilled to be a part of the ride. Ravel's "Bolero" took the long crescendo to new extremes. Your presentations should not last as long as that piece of music, but you should sit through it in it's entirety at least once in life to appreciate its power. Regular, consistent acceleration of tempo, and an incremental increase in volume make crescendo a great tool and necessary skill in making presentations.

Rhythm

Early in my speaking career (now over 19 years and counting), any of the distractions listed earlier in this chapter would throw me completely off my pace, and my rhythm would be lost. I would have practiced, rewrote, and listened to what I was going to say, and in what order, and around what humor, only to learn painfully that I had left something out—the other people in the room.

It was painful for me to have to learn to allow these people's comments to pepper the conversation. Then, I had an epiphany. I needed to stop using the "I am the expert and you should listen" lecture approach. A presentation needs to be more of a *conversation*.

Call and response—I ask a question, someone in the room answers, she feels as though she is part of it, I get her to buy in, and then other people are looking for their opportunity to put in their two cents worth. Now, almost instantly, I have the audience interested. Next, I add the technique of using people's names when they speak up. I know of nothing more pleasing to the human ear than the sound of our own name. By asking a question or two at the outset, the people in the room acknowledge why I am standing in front and mentally decide to allow me to continue.

The one question I ask early in every presentation is, "What do we want to get out of the time we spend together?" This starts a rhythm of interaction. It gives me a sense of pace and responsiveness of the group. It tells me how to proceed.

Tone

Tone can apply to two things:

1. Your voice
2. The presentation

If you are determined to close the deal at the end of your presentation, you must make it easy for your audience. You must walk them through familiar territory, and you must invite them to a specific action at the end. Tell them that after the meeting there will be an opportunity for questions and to discuss the next step. If you want people to walk away from your presentation with the thought of taking a specific action, you must make that action clear.

A Painful Lesson

Early in my selling career, a friend of mine and I cold-called a series of buildings on Ventura Boulevard in Los Angeles. We walked in off the street, went floor to floor, and boldly entered enemy territory. *It was great fun.*

Our objective was to see if we could get an appointment with a sales manager, to come back later to try to sell him our sales training. Cedric and I were shocked by one office manager who responded, "I was just about to start a sales meeting—you want to present to the group?"

We were thrilled and horrified at the same time. We had not expected to be invited in on the spot. Confidently, and with great aplomb, we walked in, and did our thing. I got up and spoke about our concepts and structures for about eight minutes, and then I turned it over to my friend. This is when the tone of the conversation we had failed to have reared its ugly head. Cedric got up, stood in front of the group, and said, "We are ready to take orders."

I can still hear and feel the silence that permeated that room for about nine seconds. The sales manager could not stand it anymore, so he cleared his throat, got up, and said, "Well, thanks for coming in," as enthusiastically as he could. Cedric and I slinked out of that office with nothing but our pride because we had not decided what tone we wanted to set in the meeting. If we wanted them to buy recordings of our training sessions, we should have been aware of that. If we wanted to be invited back to do a half-day seminar at a later sales meeting, we should have known that as well. The painful, irrevocable bottom line was that we blew it.

The other aspect of tone draws on some of the other concepts—rhythm, crescendo, silence, harmony—because they all work in concert (no pun intended) to establish the tone of your voice, the tone of your delivery, and the tone that is being received by your audience.

Tempo

Tempo has to do with speed, and it also is interrelated with rhythm. It is not the same thing because various rhythms may be delivered in multiple tempos. Ever hear an old pop song redone with a blues or reggae feel? The tempo is different and that changes the feel, which changes the perception.

Improvisation

Jazz musicians are in awe of the sheer technical skill and knowledge displayed by their classical colleagues. Classical musicians marvel at how musicians performing a jazz band can feel each other changing tempo or rhythm, and build a dynamic crescendo, without a conductor, and without a piece of music in front of them.

The ability to improvise is a key attribute of The Ultimate Sales Manager, and it is essential for you and your folks to develop great presentation skills. If you rely on technology and have everything exciting about your presentation saved in PowerPoint but the projector refuses to cooperate, you must be able to present your ideas, case, meeting, or call to action with just your voice, knowledge, and body language.

I have presented difficult and intricate concepts with a flip chart and markers to people all over the world, and the beauty and comfort in that is that I can stand up and present my topic at a moments' notice, anywhere at any time. This paragraph is not about me, neither is it an indictment of presentation problems. It says that it would be healthy (and very impressive) for more people to walk into a presentation, turn off the computer, and present a compelling case because they were passionate and knowledgeable.

Your presentation is not in your laptop. It is in your heart and in your head. If you believe that you have salespeople who do not have their heart in their work, please figure out how you can make up their revenue with someone else sitting at their desk. Improvisation shows command of the material, a willingness to engage instead of lecture, and it shows that you really are the person to whom attention should be paid.

Audience Response

People applaud at the end of jazz solos because it is part of the jazz music culture. It allows the musician and audience to have something fleeting, unique, irretrievable, and memorable together. These sound like tall orders for a simple sales presentation, but they are worth reaching for because you will distinguish yourself from the competition by doing something that no one else does. This means you must take risks: Have your audience be a part of the presentation. (Do not insist that people save questions to the end. You must be prepared and professional so that your presentation is productive, and the people it needs to be productive for are the ones sitting in the chairs.)

In my travels, people who also speak professionally have told me that my approach is at once alarming and dangerous. The first time I heard this, I was shocked. "Why do you say that?" I asked. They answered, "Because you actually encourage people to ask you questions—to interrupt you—I would never want that. It kills my rhythm, and it could get in the way of me getting through all of my material."

I like living a bit dangerously. No, I am not a jet test pilot (nor do I travel down the Amazon looking to pick a fight with a crocodile) but I do like the edge of having to know my material so well, that I had better be prepared for any question that comes up. Can you be the expert on everything your company offers, every eventuality of engaging your service, or every feature of your product? Probably not, but you can make presentations often, and the audience responses you encounter will inform how you present over time. You want audience response. It can be perceived as a buy sign.[1]

Emotion

Don't get carried away. Make sure that you are prepared, productive, and professional, and *never* knock your competition. Quite simply, it makes you look small. Most people are averse to this technique of making slight comments against someone else because it is unethical and petty. I cannot stomach the approach, and I abandon the salesperson. This scenario happened to me recently. I was on the phone with a local company, investigating their service. I am going to purchase that service from someone, and I was learning about this particular provider.

As the salesperson was explaining their service, I asked, "What is the key difference between you and the nationally known providers?" He responded, "Well, we saw that they weren't doing it right. We basically stole the idea right away from them, and off we went with the profit, which is good for you." He was telling me how bad, unprofessional, and unresponsive the other company was. I really could not take it and told him, "I've heard enough, thank you." The line was silent for a moment, and I repeated, "Thank you." He responded with surprise (maybe shock): "Uhhh. Okay, thank *you*." He was surprised, and the call ended.

What you feel about an idea, a competitor, or anything not relevant to the issue at hand for your presentation is completely irrelevant. How you make the people in the room feel about their opinions is where presentation skills become difficult. How can you discuss anything without informing the discussion with your opin-

---

[1] A buy sign is simply and only an indication of interest. I will take this over no indication of interest, however: It does not mean they are ready to buy, it is a sign that they *may* buy.

ions? I want you to be positive, excited, enthusiastic, but not evangelical about your topic. Emotions run high in the selling world. Keep yours in check.

Technique

Learn how to use your body, hands, eyes, voice, language, and mind all at once. Then you will have mastered presentation skills. In the meantime, the two most influential steps I have ever taken to develop my technique were:

1. Joining Toastmasters
2. Videotaping myself making a presentation

Toastmasters

If you are not familiar with Toastmasters, and you are a sales manager, or want to be one some day, then look into what they have to offer. It is not a quick fix. It is not easy. It *is*, however, the most supportive, logical, unbiased environment you will ever encounter. Go to their web site, http://www.toastmasters.org, and find a few local clubs. If you are in a major metropolitan area, I guarantee there are a dozen that meet within a few blocks of your office or home. If you are in suburbia you may have to drive a bit to get to one, but the important lesson here is, *go to one.*

You can usually attend one meeting free of charge, and get a sense of what the experience, and the objectives are all about. You can try a few on for size, to see which one of them fit your schedule, personality, and goals.

I joined a Toastmasters club at the urging of a former manager, and I cannot thank him enough. I thought I would go there and get leads. What I got was an education, a profound development of my raw abilities, and the opportunity to grow with people who had similar goals, but who came from a variety of professions and ways of doing things. One of the most fascinating men was a comedy producer. At one time, he had worked for the comedian Gallagher (maybe you have seen him smash watermelons as part of his act). I remember him because he was so good at leading the meetings. He was a member because he wanted to learn to improvise in front of a business audience, and the way he developed during the time we were members together was very satisfying to watch.

Videotape

I would prefer that you not videotape a practice session. Instead, videotape yourself live, in front of an audience. Make sure that you are in a room where your voice records well, and if you can, see if you can have the camera behind audience members. This allows you to observe what people are doing while you speak. Fascinating is one word that describes the first time I saw a videotape of myself speaking in front of a group. Horrified is another word. Wanting to climb deep into my chair, and disappear there forever, is another strong emotional memory. And I was watching the tape alone.

Videotape is great because it is affordable and easy to use. Videotape is unforgiving, because it is unwaveringly accurate. It sugarcoats *nothing*. Ultimately, it tells the truth.

♦

You and your team can grow in surprising ways, if several people enroll and participate in Toastmasters (even if you go to different clubs), if you practice together, and offer constructive feedback, if you videotape presentations, and if you practice.

You, The Ultimate Sales Manager, can start to identify people who could potentially demonstrate future leadership through this process. You can help your folks gain more confidence, and you can *close more deals.*

Once your team cold-calls regularly, they will be called out to make more presentations. At many of these meetings, they will have the opportunity to close business. We further explore closing in Chapter 14.

14

CLOSING TECHNIQUES ALL SALESPEOPLE SHOULD KNOW

ABOUT CLOSING

The members of your sales team must ask for business often, subtly, directly, consistently, and professionally. When one of your reps comes in with a new piece of business, it is because they have done a monumentally important thing: They closed the prospect and made him a customer. This is great news.

What we need to keep in mind is that you are sending people out to battle each day, and you want to make sure they follow the precepts of the Sales Geneva Convention:

♦ Every prospect will be treated with respect, regardless of whether she buys from the competition or us.
♦ Never disparage the competition, especially if the prospect is currently buying from that competitor.
♦ The deal you are offering is not the only one available out there, so you need to keep your eyes and ears open to new

offerings, promotions, price differentials, and any other way the competition might be taking business away from you.

♦ If a prospect decides not to buy from you, thank him for his time and then leave. Quietly, quickly, and politely.

♦ When someone does buy from us, she is transferring value from her budget to us. Treat this with respect and appreciation. People have choices. Don't give them a reason (or reasons) to go elsewhere.

CLOSES YOU SHOULD TEACH YOUR TEAM

There are numerous tactics and techniques salespeople have developed to facilitate the closing of a sale. These sound dangerously like confidence schemes, designed to relieve people of their poorly guarded wallet. Yet, they are time-tested, effective, and honorable closing techniques. The Ultimate Sales Manager can walk his sales force through these techniques on a moment's notice. The Ultimate Sales Manager is a constant student of his profession, and is not only interested in the newest idea (which has value), but he understands the history of the profession as well.

The Take-Away Close

Let's pretend that you are a buyer of Gigabats (something absolutely necessary for the smooth and profitable operation of your business). Several people call on you annually to sell you Gigabats, and you have used different vendors for different reasons. In this scenario, I also decide to call on you, and we sit in your office, talking about how you use them. At this point, I get you to do most of the talking, and I learn a few things about your choices, your preferences, and what has worked for you in the past.

I then say, "Well, based on what you have told me so far, the Gigabats that we *offer* (try not to say *sell*) could probably fit your requirements, and the pricing is very much in line with how we structure things for orders of the size and frequency you mentioned, but honestly, ours may not be for you."

I then sit in silence, while you try to figure out why not. You likely then ask yourself, "Why not?"

At this moment, I have attempted to take something away from you, and specifically what I have attempted to take is the choice of whether you should buy these Gigabats from me. You, being human, will not like that. You feel a sense of loss, possibly a loss of control of the event, and so you sit up straight, and prepare to argue with me about whether you should buy from me. You present a case, and you are close to placing an order, when I surrender. My palms out, my shoulders in submission, I say, "All right, all right—if you insist, I will sell them to you."

This is the take-away close. There are other ways to get to a similar experience, yet they all revolve around removing the decision making from the other person, without being blatant, rude, or condescending. Selling is an honorable profession, and this is an honorable closing technique. I used it as part of an interview once, and the interviewer would not let me out of his office without making me an offer. I even negotiated my new salary on the spot.

By saying, "I may not be the guy for you," I attempted to "take away" his option to disqualify me as a candidate for a position for which I was (I admit now) marginally qualified.

The Puppy Dog Close

Another classic closing technique that every sales manager should know is the puppy dog close. This is similar to the take-away, yet with a twist. You have to deliver this technique with a smile.

Let's pretend you are the parent of a young girl, and you make the mistake of bringing her into a pet store. Let's say the proprietor has an AKC registered puppy for sale. The owner of the store does not speak to you—she hands the puppy to the girl, and encourages her to name it. Guess who is walking out of the pet store that day with a puppy? You may attempt to turn the puppy down, but those of us who may have trouble saying no to our daughters can certainly relate to this experience.

The Ben Franklin Close

Ben Franklin is almost a mythical character to me because his creative juices and output ran full steam very late into his life. He may have been reviled by some of the other founding fathers for his success in France, or his attitude toward international affairs, but he was also very well known for creativity, and most of all, curiosity. I find that salespeople who are truly curious about the world around them find ways to be creative, and as a result, more successful.

As a sales manager, you want to give your folks all the tools you can. At your next local sales meeting, walk them through the Ben Franklin. It is rumored that old Ben was very judicious in his decision making, and he tried to keep emotion out of his most critical decisions. (At least that is what the myth is—I am not a historian, and for all I know, this might be more appropriately called the John Adams.) But since I was taught this as the Ben Franklin, I'm sticking with my story. Ben used a very simple physical exercise for deciding either "for" or "against" an idea or proposal.

He would draw an oversized "T" on a piece of paper, as indicated below, with the headings you see there.

For	Against
1.	1.
2.	2.
3.	3.
4.	4.
5.	5.

And so on. Once he made a complete list of all of the reasons for or against, he would simply go with the side that had more reasons, based on his clear thinking.

The challenge in this exercise is to take the most objective view of the situation, its implications and predicted outcomes, to be sure that we avoid editorializing, and breaking some reasons into sub-reasons, just to fill out a list.

How do we use this as a closing technique? I'm glad you asked. Sit across the table from a prospect, and ask her for a piece of paper and a pen. Now, you must be prepared for the fact that you might actually assist your prospect in ruling against buying from you, but selling is not about getting every deal—it is about serving your clients and your employer. This means that not everyone with money and willingness to buy should be your customer.

Walk her through the Ben Franklin technique. Draw a simple T on the paper, and write For and Against on top. Ask the tough questions first. Have her verbalize one of the reasons not to buy from you. It may not be fun, but it will be educational, and that is much more valuable at this point.

Once she is comfortable telling you a reason (or a few reasons) *not* to buy from you, get her thinking on the other track. Ask her to describe some reasons that she should buy from you. This will be more fun for both of you, and it will get her to see the sheer number of reasons why she should go in that direction.

Invite her to continue after you leave. Say, "You can look at this later, and really give it some thought." Many times, she is so involved because everything on the paper came out of her mouth that she wants to see where the process goes. She insists that you continue. (I *love* it.)

Or after just a few of these ideas are written down, put the pen down, and ask, "So, how long after you finish this should we speak again?" and move as if you are planning to leave. (Subtle repeat of the take-away—she will think, even if only for a moment, "Where is he *going?*") Many times, people will want to finish the list right in front of you. Others may want to take the list to a boss, coworker, or committee. But the best experience is when the prospect crumples the list up into a ball, and then asks, "Where is your order form?" Or says, "Let me get you a purchase order number."

Any subtle, clear, specific step that prospects take toward buying from you is the result of logic, as well as a nonmanipulative approach. This solidifies in their mind that you are someone who holds their interests and concerns in high esteem and that you attach a priority to their comfort and desire to do business with you.

The Fear of Loss Close

Now, since I have tried many of these closes, I am allowed to editorialize. I personally do not like this approach. It is important for you to be familiar with (and to share with your team) which closes you endorse and which you do not.

As such, I will now describe the Fear of Loss Close. In this scenario, you and I are in a conversation about my Gigabats. You have engaged providers for similar services in the past, and you have shared with me that you have a budget, and as of yet, you have not committed that budget. This sounds like an opportunity for me to continue to sell. Until I get the deal there is still a chance that someone else will close you, and that is unacceptable to me. I am a competitor. I want to win.

With this in mind, I want to get you to act as soon as I can. Therefore, I will speak to you about the limited availability of my service after a certain date because our resources will have been committed to *some* organization, maybe yours, maybe your competitors'. If you are like me, and you like to compete, you want to know that your decisions, plans, and actions take your competitor out of the arena. I suggest (without saying it blatantly) that hesitation on your part spells opportunity for your competitor. At this point, I have instilled a modicum of fear in you.

Most people in a buying-decision capacity are not going to be afraid, but there will be a tinge of nervousness about the repercussions of a missed opportunity. By creating the notion that an opportunity will be lost, I instill the Fear of Loss sensation and motivator, and as a result, you buy from me.

I said at the outset that I personally am not a subscriber to this approach, but I must, in the interest of full disclosure, tell you that I have seen it applied with great effect (the prospect bought on the spot) in many situations, by other people with whom I have sold.

My problem with it is that it employs a bit of undue, borderline inappropriate influence. Use this as you see fit. A very successful sales book launched a consulting career for a psychiatrist some years ago, with references to the fact that by analyzing people's situations, you could speak to them about the consequences of *not* buying, which would result in the prospect feeling as though they could not live without whatever was being sold to them. It works, but that doesn't mean I use it.

As The Ultimate Sales Manager, it is up to you to set the tone for how your team sells, person to person, and prospect to prospect. In the same way that you are on display on the sales floor every day, your salespeople are on display either over the phone or out in the world. What they do reflects on you and your company. What do you want your team to be known for? What is the image you would like portrayed, if they were to make a movie about life working on your sales team, or as part of your sales force? In effect, your image is walking around with every one of your salespeople. What do you want your buying population to think or see?

JOHN'S PERSONAL FAVORITES

Since I am editorializing to great extent on the closing techniques I tend *not* to use, let me walk you through some of the ones I *love* to use.

The Assumptive Close

Even with all of the jokes surrounding the word "assume," I find this to be one of the smoothest, least obvious, yet effective closes in my personal arsenal. With the Assumptive Close, I get to the point in the conversation where the prospect has asked many questions, and it appears to me as though I have answered satisfactorily.

Remember: Each direct question that a prospect asks is a sign of interest. With each question and inquiry to which I respond, the prospect looks for more verification that he or she should buy from me. With each forward step, I relax more, because now *the prospect* is driving the conversation. This works for me, because now I can relax and enjoy what we are doing.

The Assumptive Close is played like this.

The prospect has investigated, assessed, and examined the offer. After a brief silence, I ask a question that assumes the sale has been made, such as "Where do you want the first order shipped?" Variations on this include:

◆ "Who will be on-site to accept the first delivery?"
◆ "What address do I send the purchase order to?"
◆ "I have your address here—what is the *billing* address?"
◆ "How soon after you move in do you want to begin this service?"

The basic tenet of the Assumptive Close is that by definition, you have assumed that the prospect has bought. The hazard in using this close is that you must also make sure that you have an actual commitment, not just an address.

The What's Next? Close

Finally, the closing technique that I employ most often is almost invisible. I tell people that I have not actually asked for an order or an appointment in 15 years, and they look at me as if I were crazier than I actually am. I love to call this final closing technique the "What's Next?" Close. It is so simple, so elegant, and so powerful, that when I use it in the presence of other people, they walk away, wondering how I closed the person we were pitching.

Here it is.

When you feel a lull in the conversation, and you feel as though you have addressed their questions, and given them ample time to decide if they should buy from you. Ask, "So, what do we do next?" The closing ratio (amount of times I employ it compared to the amount of times I get the business) is at least 75 percent.

Stunning. Powerful. Ultimate.

◆

In Chapter 15, we look at tying many of these concepts together, sending you out into the world to make a difference.

15

EXPECTATION
MANAGEMENT

What you think your team knows and what they actually plan to do are often two very different things. With expectation management, you combine all of your skills to communicate with, interact with, and motivate each person on your team, setting expectations in a realistic manner.

Recently, I sat in on a regional meeting with a leader of a sales force. During the meeting, the leader discussed growth, development, and opportunities that the company was interested in offering employees who fulfilled certain criteria. The leader looked around the room and asked the group, "Are any of you ready for this?"

An uncomfortably awkward silence followed. Some of the attendees were convinced (based on previous experience) that the company would not promote from within. Others were convinced that they were the perfect candidate for one or more of the new openings, and so they didn't think it was necessary to raise their hands. Yet a smaller group was wondering why anything like the new positions would be of any interest to anyone in the room because they knew they were currently underperforming. I have all of this as reliable fact because after this meeting, I conducted one-on-one coaching with each person.

What surprised me most was how many people were less than accurate when describing what they thought the leader was saying. His question ("Are any of you ready for this?") was perceived differently by almost every person.

To a few, the question appeared as a challenge, as if the leader meant to say, "I am convinced that none of you are ready for this, so it is a given that we will go outside the company for this new crop of leaders." Others took it as a confirmation that since they were convinced that they were individually ready, it was unnecessary for them to raise their hands during that meeting. The most fascinating discussion was with the leader of this group, later in the day.

He told me how frustrated he was that no one raised their hands—that not one person had taken the risk of expressing interest in front of others. My reaction to the leader's question was that it seemed like a challenge rather than a call to action, almost as though he was saying, "I don't think any of you are ready, but I would like to know if you think you are." This is not what he meant, but that is not the issue at hand. What is important is the message that the audience received.

You cannot wave a wand and get people to think, act, or react the way you think they should. I have learned this through a painful process called trial and multiple error. However, by being very specific in what I say, I draw on all of my talents and skills to make my intentions and message as clear as possible.

Expectation management is not a euphemism for expectation understanding. Nor does it translate into expectation achievement. Out of everything that you will build into your management approach because of this book, expectation management has the potential to cause you the greatest headaches.

CLARITY IS THE KEY

During my tenure as a training manager, I was asked one of the most difficult questions any manager ever asked me: "Why would you do that?" My supervisor was frustrated with some decision I had made in his absence, and I apparently had not lived up to his expectations. Unfortunately, I did not know what he expected, so I did what I thought was the right thing at that moment.

If you want your team to think on their feet, to solve problems, to be mentally flexible and emotionally stable, you must make your expectations clear. The Ultimate Sales Manager sets very clear expectations, and stays close to the action, to inspect what is expected.

Frank Phillips, the president of RN Network (a staffing company for traveling nurses), located in Fort Lauderdale, Florida, is a reliable and credible authority because he started his career at a sales desk. After working his way up, Frank started a company in the same industry. As president, everyone in the organization reports to him.

When I interviewed Frank, I asked, "How is managing salespeople different from managing people in other job functions?" Frank responded:

> I think that it might be tougher than others because more people in sales want to do things their own way. It might work great for them, but it may not work great for the organization as a whole. They might sell or work in a way to positively impact their commission strategically, but it may negatively impact the organization. This is tricky, and here's why.
>
> Good salespeople are looking at "What's in it for me?" (this is part of what makes them good in sales—they are opportunistic). What they will do to secure deals may maximize their individual compensation, but it may not add to the bottom line, so we are always looking at our compensation plans to serve both.
>
> As far as accountability and setting expectations my process has always been:
> - ◆ Set both an expectation and an example.
> - ◆ Do not ask people to do something that I would not do.
> - ◆ Give people ways to get what they want, and satisfy the expectation.

Many times, it is a matter of rolling up your sleeves and getting involved. I am a strong believer in management by example. I may not sell every day, but I *can* sell. I do it with and for salespeople. I have personal selling experience. I did not just magically appear with the title "president." I have been on the front lines of selling. I made my living selling the staffing of physicians. I have sold in health care staffing since 1990. I started by working a desk, worked my way into a management position, and six years into my career, I had an opportunity to start a company, thanks to some investment from others.

I want to be very clear—I ask for daily activities for which the salespeople are accountable. How long someone has been in a particular position determines what I expect of him or her. I do not hold someone with tenure of one month accountable for the same things that someone who has been here three years would be expected to do. We break down the day into certain activities, and the different job function (recruiting, client sales, or consulting) determines what the activities are.

Recruiters are asked to do a minimum of 70 outbound calls a day. We do not dictate percentages of how many might be cold. These calls may be relationship development, as well. Recruiters with over a year should have three "submissions" per day. This means that they need to have three nurses that they are submitting to hospitals for opportunities. Three a day—it's the mantra.

The other thing they are responsible for is identifying new nurses, and getting them into our database. We have measurement tools that indicate the number of calls, the talk time, the number of submissions made, the number of nurses on interview, and number of nurses "locked in" (on assignment) for a particular day.

We do not track the number of nurses hired because our salespeople have no control over that. They *do* have control over how many they submit in a given day, and that is what we are looking for—that is what we hold them accountable for.

As far as revenue dollars, we have not taken it to that extent because revenue is based on the contract rates that someone else has negotiated that with the hospital. That comes from a separate sales function (the regional sales director).

Recruiters do have some control over what the nurse is paid, so we look at a gross margin line, as opposed to bottom line. I am definitely interested in holding people accountable for what they do.

Frank focuses on the details that are instrumental in being an effective manager. The Ultimate Sales Manager balances data with understanding, driving, and interacting with the people who create the data. Frank continued:

For a senior player, we might have different conversations about activity levels not being met. If submissions are not what they need to be, I will first look at her dials. If they appear to be in line, then I will look a step deeper, and try to see who she is calling. Is she prospecting or stirring the pot? If I can see that she is prospecting and not hitting her numbers, then something is wrong. It should not happen in our market.

We need to keep people listed with us. This is where we compete, and it's tough. Travel nurses are in high demand, and they know it. They get to be in the driver's seat. We have to be good at selling what we offer. The good news is that we may offer a few things that other companies don't. One thing that is challenging for us is that we have business coming in the door every day, but we also have deals fall apart at the last minute, for a variety of reasons.

I expect to be able to hit our corporate goals, and we know how many new hires it takes in a given period to maintain our corporate trend goal. Every week, we have people beginning assignments, and we have people going onto new assignments, so I have a specific net number of new starts per week, in order to serve the corporate goal. We know there will be "fall-off," or people who are scheduled to start, but, for whatever reason, do not. I have to add new salespeople to take us to the next level.

JK: So, "vision precedes everything"?

FP: Absolutely.

JK: What was the transition like going from being a desk salesperson to running an organization?

FP: I was all of a sudden responsible for someone other than myself. I think about making decisions from the perspective that my decisions not only impact my family—they now impact the families of the people who work here. I carry the weight of the world, because every day people are looking to me to make sure that they have security.

JK: How important is it that you as a sales manager have personal selling experience?

FP: I think it is very important, and I do not think that the people who are super star salespeople will be the best candidate for a sales management position. I learned a lot in playing baseball in school about team play, and recognizing that although I may not have been the star player, I did learn how to be a fairly decent coach. My sense is that good sales managers have rarely been the top-performing salesperson. Top-performing salespeople may be too selfish to be a good manager. This "selfishness" makes them successful. They have a singular focus—to close a deal. Sales managers look at it as, "It would be good for the company for us to win it."

There are two growth avenues—I could have stayed on a sales desk. I decided to pursue a management track, and I like taking people from ground zero and helping turn them into people who live a lifestyle they would never have realized without becoming better in sales. There are people who work for me who earn more money than me, and that is okay. It's okay for a few reasons:

- I had the opportunity (and still have the choice at any time) to go back into sales, and run a desk, and earn more money.
- Their earning that money ensures that I have a job.
- I like being a part of creating that change in their lives.

Sales management is the impossible profession, because if you look up "management" in the dictionary, I am not sure you can apply that to what I do. I believe sales management is better equated to either being a coach, or the conductor of an orchestra. I have all the various instruments represented, and I have to find a way to bring them all together and to create beautiful music. That may sound romantic, but it communicates how much I love what I do.

The world may not think about the president of a company as a creative person, but it requires tremendous creativity to draw music out of that orchestra every day.

Frank is fortunate. He loves what he does. He surrounds himself with people who are committed. He provides a valuable service that touches people and families he has never met.

PRACTICE BEING REALISTIC

One discovery I have made during my years of selling, managing, and living is that however hard we try to manage other people's expectations, it is nearly impossible to actually do so. I can prepare people for certain eventualities, I can "overcommunicate" as we were instructed in the military, but what I do or say is nowhere near as important as what people walk away from the conversation thinking. To them, you are seen as either an advocate or an impediment, an ally or an enemy.

AFTER VISION, SPECIFIC ACTIONS

My personal approach to each new team I created or inherited was to open the first meeting by asking the team what they expected of me. I would open the conversation by stating that I was looking forward to being a part of a great working environment. Then, I would ask, "So, what do you expect from me, as your manager?"

The responses would invariably start in a slow, even halting, manner, but as is typical of salespeople (and people in general) once the door was opened, they were thrilled to rush inside with their two or fifty cents worth.

This was a great exercise for the group, and with each new person I would hire—it would set and foster a tone of openness, and one that established the sales manager (*me*) as a listener.

The toughest and most productive part of this exercise was that I would not limit the amount of time that people were afforded to speak. This gave me the chance to learn much about the interaction of the group, and the dynamic of the team, just by what people choose to bring up. During this, I made a point of jotting down key things that were said, making particular note of things that were mentioned more than once.

Then, once the dialog seemed to have run its course, I presented a specific, short list of what I expected in return from the team. Often, people saw this as a logical step. Others took offense, feeling as though I had baited them. After I delivered my measured, specific, and brief list, I would ask, "How does that sound?"

This was the opportunity for the de facto leader to take me to task, or any individuals who felt hostile just because I was "the new guy," and had not had the opportunity to get to know me, learn from me, or get any help closing a deal from me to express their opinions.

Typically, however, it was a great exercise because it illustrated to my team that I planned to ensure that *they* were heard first. They got to speak *before* I did. It did not seem as though I was "laying down the law" within my first few minutes with the team.

Since we cannot control what people think or feel, and we can drive ourselves crazy trying to understand erratic, emotional behavior by using a scale based on logic, it was freeing for me to get this discussion out of the way up front. After this initial discussion, I would then tell them that I had taken specific notes and that I looked forward to hearing from them individually in the future to compare notes and track progress. I would end the meeting with a motivational story, to let them know that I intended to be part of a team that was interested in winning, and winning regularly.

A LITTLE MOTIVATION

When I first took over a team of advertising sales professionals, I told one of my favorite stories. In Charles Garfield's book titled *Peak Performers* (New York: Avon, 1986), there is an account of the American space program from the 1960s, and how important it was that everyone involved, regardless of their role, experience, or education, was a contributor to the overall cause. (I *really* love this story.)

Mr. Garfield was at Grumman, the engineering and aeronautics firm on Long Island, walking around with some of the executives, when he saw a man sweeping the floor. He asked the man, "What are you doing?" The man replied, "I'm putting a man on the moon."

This commitment, communication, and cooperation struck me as something that I wanted to instill in every team with which I was involved. When I told the story to these advertising sales professionals, one started to wipe a tear from her eye. This reaction, this *impact*, is what I am looking for as a manager, a leader, as someone who brings about change and unlocks the potential of other people.

Getting people revved up is great fun (and a great challenge) because you get people committed to a cause, but make sure that you find a way to manage them (get the most out of them) without getting in their way.

ULTIMATELY ATTAINABLE

Many of the comments in this book are geared toward the "ideal." We are interested in your ability to be measured and perceived as The Ultimate Sales Manager as an obtainable future condition. I believe that it is attainable, and I offer no apology for raising the bar so high.

We take that lofty goal and objective, and hang some real meat on it by hearing from some very informed, professional, productive people who prepared for their time with me by looking over the working outline of this book, choosing the concepts and assignments critical to sales management, and addressing those. Let's see what Shari Franey has to say.

Shari and I were both selling in the staffing and employment industry when we met at an American Staffing Association convention. She is the president and principal of the Performance Group, a placement and training company based in Harrisburg, Pennsylvania. We talked for quite a while about accountability. Shari says:

> The Ultimate Sales Manager holds salespeople accountable. Accountability can be one of the largest challenges. "Herding cats" is

similar to trying to work with people who see themselves as some-one who is out in the forefront, perhaps your shining star, or even a Lone Ranger, and having him feel as though he is accountable, and that he is a part of a team. The Ultimate Sales Manager also seeks to grow others, and guide them into a better place for them-selves and the company.

From the very beginning, we see our salespeople as leaders. When I converse with them, I treat them as leaders. As such, we do not want them out in the world playing by their own rules. But in the position of a leader, they will have expectations from oth-ers. They are the reputation of the company—they cannot act as if their actions have no ramifications.

JK: Vision precedes everything?

SF: That's right. We begin at the interview stage with conver-sations about leadership. We have an internal leadership in-stitute in which we ask our salespeople to participate. In our industry, we refer to our different locations as branches. Each branch has a branch manager, and a sales-person. The salesperson is a coleader in the branch. We cannot have people off doing things on their own; other-wise, we fail. We want them to succeed, and that means we want them to be a part of a team.

I think what we have tried to do, as far as accountability, is make clear what the expectations are. By planting that, and drumming it home through discipline, we want our salespeo-ple to live out that role. The sales job has guidelines.

We have weekly branch meetings, and the salesperson needs to contribute to that meeting, by sharing her sales activity. In conjunction with that, she is in conversation with the entire branch, regarding what she is doing. And she needs to know what is going on in the branch, so we know what we need to tweak, change, go after, whatever, and then there are minutes sent to me from the branch meetings. I like to see those minutes because they give me insight into how the branch manager and the salesperson are working together.

One of the ways that I stay involved as an owner, and part of the sales team is I do daily phone calls with my salespeople. Even though we are separated geographically, I can ask on a daily basis about activity, and how things go. We have a standard of conducting "20-Call Bursts™" (a Klymshyn creation).

If my salespeople tell me in the morning that they are going to do a call burst, or go on appointments, then at the end of the day, or the following morning, I can ask them how things went.

You can also see if these things are being discussed with the team in the branch. We want and encourage everyone to work together, and I expect my salespeople to help and encourage the branch people to be salespeople as well.

The person who supervises salespeople is the sales manager. The role of the sales manager has a tremendous amount of contact. I asked Shari: "What are the challenges with having salespeople be accountable?" She answered:

The biggest challenge for the sales manager is to have his people understand the importance of accountability. Salespeople tend to have an innate sense of competition, and they want to go out and play the game, without having to feel as though they need to check in with the coach. That is why it is essential that the sales manager begin the relationship by explaining why important regular contact, regular discussion with the salesperson about activity, strategy, and attainment is so important.

We work in partnership with our client companies, we work in partnership with our inside staff, and the salesperson and the sales manager have to work in partnership to get the most out of the relationship. Partnership includes accountability.

I, as the sales manager, need to be available to my salespeople. If we say that we are going to do something, we have to make sure that we do it. Discipline is a huge part of the overall relationship, in that self-discipline means that you know what you need to do, and you do it. If no one ever looks at activity, or does not look in the computer to see what I have recorded, then there is no reason for me to do it. Sales management means that you track activity, and people know that you are part of the process by examining what they do.

If someone does not record information on a client conversation properly, and that client calls the office, then no one knows the context of the conversation. Management is about what is best for the clients and, as a result, for the company. If no one looks at documentation or record keeping, it will not continue. You cannot expect what you do not inspect.

Sales Management is helping a salesperson become the best that he or she can be, which helps to push the company into a healthier, sounder place. If you are doing your job as a sales manager, you want to help someone achieve his or her best. Sales managers who are looking for a situation where the success is all about them are not going to succeed.

Momentum is a great thing, and it can be a powerful force because people want to be around winners. They want to work in a winning branch. Sales managers want to help salespeople become more well rounded. It is more than just sales skill; it also is about leadership ability.

A salesperson assuming a leadership stance is a huge factor in the success of our company. When people talk about what "the company" should do, they need to get a clue as to the fact that they are not separate from the company—they *are* the company.

I am also a big fan of going out on calls with salespeople because when you go out as a salesperson, and you are with someone else, you speak more deliberately, you tend to stand up a bit straighter, and you get to evaluate and compare what you are doing to what other people do. You cannot operate in a vacuum. When salespeople are out on a call with other salespeople, they are more aware of what they do, what they say, and how they carry themselves.

We often do team selling, and sales blitzes, where there are prizes for the person who brings back the most contacts or business cards. This is designed to do a few things:

♦ It is fun.
♦ It hones their sales skills a bit.
♦ It brings people together who might not see each other all the time.
♦ You have blitzed the whole area, so you get a lot out of it.

It focuses people on the *generation* of *activity*.

Our salespeople are required to send new account information to me and to our accounting department. They have to calculate margins, and they need to enter it into the system, or we cannot fulfill anything. Discipline is important because the work that we do is too interconnected to have someone in the group who wants to be a Lone Ranger.

MISTAKES WE HAVE MADE

I asked Shari, and several other sales managers, leaders, and coaches in preparation for this book, what they felt some common mistakes that they (or managers they knew) had made. Here is a brief list of their thoughts:

- Thinking that salespeople are continually motivated.
- Thinking that salespeople can sustain their momentum.
- Thinking that their salespeople do not need nurturing or guidance.
- Thinking their salespeople are completely self-sustaining and sufficient.
- Assuming that salespeople have all the answers.
- Assuming that their salespeople have mastered the skills required to sell effectively.

And the biggest mistake of all, in my opinion:

- Changing commitments and not following through (I will visit with you on such a date, and then postponing or not making it at all).

No matter how you rationalize it, this tells the salespeople that they or their work are not priorities for you.

I asked Shari about the importance of personal sales experience and how it prepares The Ultimate Sales Manager. She responded:

Very important, from a credibility issue. How can you ask your salespeople to do something that you have never done? As a sales manager you need to be able to constantly train and coach, and grow and develop.

When we first spoke about the tenets, and Attributes of The Ultimate Sales Manager, Shari related what I mentioned in the introduction: managing salespeople is akin to "herding cats." After speaking with her at length about these ideas, I realized that if anyone could herd cats, The Ultimate Sales Manager could, and does, on a regular basis.

Strength, personality, compassion, and discipline begin to describe the experience, the requirements, and the benefits of you aspiring to, and working to become The Ultimate Sales Manager. You serve and coddle; you counsel and direct. You parent and befriend, and you see people's sales careers end. But most of all, you impact people's lives, for a long time, and in profound ways.

You are the absolute leverage point in today's economy because you make the difference in how your company generates profit, pays its bills, and impacts your community. I salute you for taking on this profession, because you increase sales and balance lives.

Appendix A

A BRIEF DISCUSSION OF ATTRIBUTES 39 THROUGH 52

When I started this book, I thought it would be an interesting idea to determine the specific attributes of the most effective and successful sales managers that I could find. The number 52 seemed appropriate, so that you, as reader and practitioner, could add one a week to your management toolkit. We have covered 38 so far. The remainder have been intimated or woven into the book via examples and comments, advice, and admonishments. Let's look at all of the remaining attributes.

Attribute 39: Hold the sales profession in high esteem.

If you don't, your people won't either.

Attribute 40: Never take credit for a salespersons' accomplishments.

You may open a conversation or close a deal, you may play a small or a large role in the success of one or more of your people, but that is your job. Standing in the spotlight must be reserved for salespeople if you want to get any further commitment, trust, or production out of them. Remember, my definition of "to manage" is *to get the most out of.* If you are a great closer, and you want the accolades for that skill, please consider returning to the sales force. You, your career, and your employer might be better served if you do.

Attribute 41: Do not attempt to teach "attitude."

I have tried this with my kids, my direct reports, even people that I have reported to—all without success. Attitude is something that either your people come to work with or they don't. Your incentives may motivate them in the short term, but the attitude required to build and maintain a career in sales is not something you, or I, or anyone interviewed for this book, can teach.

Attribute 42: Understand and apply the perpetual formula: Preparation + Professionalism = Productivity.

Attribute 43: Recognize when people go beyond the call, and find a unique way to thank or encourage them in front of their peers.

Attribute 44: Never let your salespeople see you sweat.

You have to operate with confidence, under pressure, and under many demands. But do not ever let your folks think you can't handle it or them.

Attribute 45: Maintain an even-keeled temper.

Attribute 46: Always be honest and forthright.

Attribute 47: Lead meetings with a greater concern for inspiration and education than for filling an hour.

Attribute 48: Find, hire, and keep a great assistant.

A great piece of advice—I know several managers who were promoted to vice presidents or presidents, but who kept the same person working for them because they viewed that person as part of their personal team. When you find that, cherish and honor it.

Attribute 49: Never use phrases like "these people" to separate yourself from the team.

Attribute 50: Regularly go out into the selling world with your salespeople.

Attribute 51: Recognize that the manager is there for the team, instead of the team being there for the sales manager.

Attribute 52: Sell vision all day, every day.

Remember: "Vision precedes everything."

Appendix B

52 ATTRIBUTES OF THE ULTIMATE SALES MANAGER

The Ultimate Sales Manager is effective and professional. The Ultimate Sales Manager has a sense of humor about himself, and about his work. The Ultimate Sales Manager takes what he does seriously but does not take himself too seriously.

The Ultimate Sales Manager makes the difference because she believes in her heart that who she is, what she does, and that the techniques she uses make a difference for her company, team, customers, and community.

The Ultimate Sales Manager also has a list of specific attributes that we have identified. These attributes are an amalgam of "always" admonishments, "never" directives, and great ideas culled from the combined experience and knowledge of the top minds in sales management in the early twenty-first century.

I chose 52 because I thought it would be great if you took one of these per week for the next year of your sales management life, to learn, apply, and own.

After thinking about that for a few days, I realized that as a sales manager, you are probably an overachiever by nature, and will go ahead and burn through these in about 52 business days at the most. That is fine. If you want to work through the concepts because sales management is new to you, or you are working on a project or paper that this book is research for, then I understand.

I would, however, love if you did practice the ideas you find here over an extended period. Move through your business day with one of these concepts in mind and keep track of its influence. See if anyone notices how methodical and realistic your approach toward your job is becoming.

This list can be downloaded from www.salesmanagersguide.com.

Visit this web site often for ideas, updates, and seminars offered by The Business Generator, Inc.

1. Understand and communicate consistently that "vision precedes everything."
2. Listen and interview well, and know who you are hiring.
3. Hire people you think will amaze you. Develop them into people who amaze themselves.
4. Work to maintain high morale through consistency, attitude, and compassion.
5. Never ask a salesperson to do something you have not done or would not do.
6. Attract top talent, retain team players, appreciate the people you have, do not delay in removing those who don't fit.
7. Truly know what makes each individual on your team tick.
8. Always work to earn the trust of your folks, one by one.
9. Work first to understand, before you expect to be understood.
10. Establish and maintain an environment of trust, hard work, fun, enthusiasm, and confidence.
11. Lead with the intent to elevate the team.
12. Spend time looking for a suitable replacement for yourself.
13. Understand that your job is about leadership, solving problems, and taking responsibility.

14. Have a long memory for people's accomplishments and a short memory for their transgressions.
15. Maintain the skill and aplomb to get your salespeople to go where you want them to go—and have them think they took you there.
16. Learn some things about the sales job that inspire people and encourage your folks to share them with the team.
17. Have recent, relevant personal selling experience.
18. Be 100 percent committed to helping other people win.
19. Understand that people will follow someone they think is looking out for them.
20. Make decisions as if your closest competitor is sitting on your shoulder.
21. Never delay or procrastinate when bad news must be delivered.
22. Be aware of the delivery, receipt, and perception of your message. *Always.*
23. Do not expect people who work *for* you to work *like* you.
24. Be the first to offer help or a joke, and the last to give up.
25. Never side with your folks against "the company." *You* are the company—so talk about news, changes and updates as if you fully support them, because you *must.*
26. Use uncommon ideas to forward other people's careers.
27. Always think two steps ahead.
28. Ensure that the plan a salesperson submits can be accomplished by that person with the tools at their disposal.
29. Recognize the unique skills, gifts, fears, and aspirations of each of your salespeople.
30. Recognize what your salespeople have in common, and what they do not.
31. Never chastise or berate in public or in private.
32. Inspect what you expect.
33. Know that you will be the topic of someone's dinner conversation.
34. Understand what motivates your people, and why they choose specific goals.

35. Never assume that what you think people are capable of is the same thing that they think they are capable of.
36. Maintain actions consistent with your character.
37. Be a great listener.
38. Hold the sales profession in high esteem.
39. Have the confidence and ability at any time to pick up the phone or walk into a building and make a cold call in front of your folks.
40. Never take credit for a sales persons' accomplishments.
41. Do not attempt to teach *attitude*.
42. Understand and apply the perpetual formula: Preparation + Professionalism = Productivity.
43. Recognize when people go beyond the call and find a unique way to thank or encourage them in front of their peers.
44. Never let your salespeople see you sweat.
45. Maintain an even-keeled temper.
46. Always be honest and forthright.
47. Lead meetings with a greater concern for inspiration and education than for filling an hour.
48. Find, hire, and keep a great assistant.
49. Never use phrases like "these people" to separate yourself from the team.
50. Regularly go out into the selling world with your salespeople.
51. Recognize that the manager is there for the team, instead of the team being there for the sales manager.
52. Sell vision all day, every day.

INDEX